The UK AIR FRYER COOKBOOK FOR BEGINNERS 2023

Banish Oil Forever and Embrace Healthy Eating!
Budget-Friendly & Easy-Breezy Air Fryer Recipes to
Respect Your Health and Your Body.

Emily J. Bailey

Table of Contents

Introduction

Benefits of using an air fryer

The air fryer is an appliance that typically has an egg shape, squared, with a removable basket on which the dishes to be cooked are placed.

It uses the high-temperature air cooking mechanism allowing a very healthy "fry-non-fry" of fresh food. Therefore, with the air fryer, there is no need to add oil, as the air replaces the oil and directly transfers its heat to the food. The cooking is perfect: the food remains soft inside but crunchy on the outside.

But in addition to frying without using oil at high temperatures, the air fryer also has other advantages:

- Cooking healthier and less fat foods: thanks to its innovative cooking system, the air fryer allows you to use up to 90% less fat than the classic fryer. This means eating food with less fat and, consequently, a healthier and healthier diet.

- No bad smells from frying: you can fry almost anything, saving us the bad smells of fried food.

- Time-saving and energy-saving: Thanks to its small size, cooking times are fast, and you don't need to preheat. This means lower energy consumption than the oven and a lower cost of electricity.

- Spend less time cleaning because you just need to throw the basket in the dishwasher, and you can use it again next time.

- Ease of use: it is used quickly, the base is removed and washed just as quickly.

- Multifunction: in the air fryer, you can do anything without sacrificing taste.

- Cooking speed: the cooking speed is impressive compared to a traditional oven. Most air fryers have modes for each type of meal, with a different preset timer for each, as mentioned earlier. Surely it is suitable for those who have no time to waste and do not want to spend too much time waiting for meals to be cooked.

- Frying safely: another positive aspect of the air fryer is that it allows you to fry safely without using hot oil, which could, if it accidentally meets the skin, cause burns.

Secret air fryer tips and tricks

An air fryer is an innovative tool and quite simple to use. However, some useful tips can help you use this fabulous appliance to the fullest.

Here are many useful tips for cooking with the air fryer:

- Use a minimal amount of oil, and lightly sprinkle a small amount on the food to be cooked. Do not use more than 1 tablespoon.

- Cooking with the air fryer works best with a dark, non-stick baking pan with low sides.

- Do not overcrowd the basket with food. The cooking and crunchiness process may slow down if the air cannot circulate around the food.

- Tinfoil, baking paper, and baking trays must never be placed on the bottom of the basket. This must always remain free so that the air can circulate properly.

- Grease your air fryer basket: foods will not stick to the bottom and will be crunchier at the end of cooking.

- Check the core temperature of the meat: the degrees and temperatures indicated in the recipes are indicative only. You must always carefully evaluate cooking based on your air fryer model. Not all air fryers have identical performance. Furthermore, the size, weight, and type of food also affect the result. For this reason, I recommend using a kitchen thermometer for cooking meat. Each type of meat requires different core temperatures to be adequately considered cooked, so I recommend checking with a thermometer in the center of the meat before consuming it.

- Do not overfill the air fryer. The more you fill it, the less well the air circulates inside. This consequently translates into lower performance and a bad result, so avoid overlapping food. If you want to cook several foods simultaneously, consider using the double cooking accessory you usually find in the accessory sets for air fryers. Also, avoid overfilling the basket when cooking vegetables. You risk that these produce too much steam during cooking and that they are boiled instead of crunchy.

- Always mix food. When cooking some foods, stir or turn the food. In this way, the foods you prepare will be cooked more evenly

- Do not use the fryer without a basket or grill inside the drawer. Never remove the perforated basket from the drawer or the grill. The reason is simple if you do it, you lose fast cooking because hot air no longer circulates under the food. The consequences are to prolong the cooking by almost double, so it must be avoided.

How to convert the recipes used in the oven to those of the air fryer

Once purchase an air fryer, many people ask themselves whether they can convert the recipes that are usually cooked in the oven into recipes for the air fryer.

The answer is yes, as both ovens and air fryers use the same cooking method: both fill an enclosed space with hot air, which cooks the food inside.

The most substantial difference between the two cooking methods is that the food becomes much crispier cooked in the air fryer than in the oven because the hot air that circulates around the food increases the surface temperature, making it more golden and crisper on the outside and soft inside.

To convert oven recipes to the air fryer, you need to use a shorter cooking time and a lower cooking temperature.

Usually, the temperature should be 10°C lower than in the oven, and the time should be lowered by 20% compared to the times used in the oven.

In any case, the advice is always to check cooking, as different models of air fryers give slightly different cooking times. Plus, just use the pause button on the machine to check cooking from time to time and flip the food for a balanced crunch on all sides.

Times for each type of food

Below you will be given a list of all the cooking times of some of the most used foods in the air fryer. Always remember that times are indicative and depend on different air fryers and the size of the food you will cook:

Meat	Time to cook
Pork ribs on the bone	25 minutes
Whole chicken	50 minutes
Hamburger	10 minutes
Chicken breast	20 minutes
Chicken wings	16 minutes
Chicken thighs	25 minutes
Roasted meat	45 minutes
Pork chops	20 minutes
Meatballs	20 minutes
Steak	15 minutes
Guinea fowl	25 minutes
Hot dog	4 minutes
Lamb's ribs	9 minutes
Sausage	20 minutes
Meatloaf	35 minutes

Fish	Time to cook
Sea bream	15 minutes
Cod	10 minutes
Salmon	15 minutes
Shrimps	8 minutes
Tuna	8 minutes

Vegetables	Time to cook
Asparagus	8 minutes
Potatoes	35 minutes
Artichokes	25 minutes
Pumpkin	15 minutes
Carrots	20 minutes
Fennels	15 minutes
Peppers	20 minutes
Eggplants	20 minutes
Zucchinis	20 minutes

Cakes and bread	Time to cook
Bundt cake	30 minutes
Cakes	25 minutes
Cupcakes	12 minutes
Muffins	15 minutes
Bread	20 minutes
Buns	15 minutes

Foods to cook and foods to avoid

Air fryers are super versatile. If you've just bought one, you're sure to wonder what the best foods are to cook in an air fryer.

Here are the foods you can cook in the air fryer:

- Frozen finger food. The air fryer is irreplaceable when it comes to preparing deep-fried frozen foods. Frozen fries, cod sticks, chicken nuggets, and potato croquettes are some of the many fried foods we can train.

- Chicken, Fish and Meat. In an air fryer, we can prepare a tender and juicy chicken; thanks to the fast cooking, the meat will not release its juices and will be very soft inside. The same goes for roasted fish or classic meatballs.

- Roasted vegetables. You can cook all kinds of vegetables: cauliflower, broccoli, eggplant, tomatoes, pumpkin, artichokes and many more. However, when using this appliance for cooking vegetables, avoid all green leafy vegetables, except if you just want to reheat them after boiling them in the pot.

- Sweet baked goods. Air fryers can be great for making desserts and single-serving desserts (small baked goods such as biscuits, apple fritters, mini strudels, bundles, and brioches). Try making cakes or donuts; you will cook something good and tasty without feeling guilty because it will be a light cooking with very low oil content.

As for the foods that cannot be cooked in the air fryer, there are:

- Rice, because to cook rice, you must immerse it in liquid and never put liquids inside an air fryer for safety reasons.

- For steamed vegetables, some air fryers have a steam setting so that they can steam vegetables. However, we do not recommend trying to steam vegetables with models that do not have this feature, as they will likely come out burnt.

- Popcorn. Making popcorn in a hot air fryer is not a good idea. The air circulating will make the beans reach everywhere, making a big mess. There is a good chance that the beans will burn or that they won't pop at all.

- Foods with too-liquid batters. The batter would end up slipping away from the food we are cooking, settling on the bottom of the basket, and leaving the food "naked" to cook. In this case, we will find on one side a basket all smeared with pastels and on the other the food deprived of the crunchy consistency of the pasta.

- Cheese. The cheese in the fryer basket, in contact with the high temperature, would end up melting, settling on the bottom and making a mess that is difficult to clean.

- Too moist foods. You can't cook gravy-laden dishes for the same reason as batters. The boiling air inside the fryer will push the liquid towards the bottom, and this will be doubly counterproductive: on the one hand, we will have food cooked without sauce and, therefore drier; on the other hand, we will have the entire basket dirty with sauce to clean up.

Breakfast

1. Apple French toast

PREPARATION TIME: 10 minutes
COOKING TIME: 10 minutes
CALORIES: 373
NUTRITIONAL VALUES: CARBS: 45 GR; PROTEINS: 8 GR; FATS: 18 GR

INGREDIENTS FOR 4 SERVINGS
- 8 slices of brioche bread
- ½ glass of milk
- 2 eggs
- 2 yellow apples
- 3 tbsp of sugar
- 1 orange
- 1 tsp of cinnamon powder
- Powdered sugar to taste

DIRECTIONS
1. Peel the apples cut them into slices and put them in a baking pan.
2. Sprinkle them with the orange juice, sugar and cinnamon and mix well.

3. Place the baking pan in the air fryer and cook at 180 ° C (356 ° F) for 10 minutes.
4. Meanwhile, put the eggs and milk in a bowl, beating them with a fork.
5. When the apples are cooked, remove them from the air fryer and set them aside.
6. Pass the slices of bread into the eggs and then put them in the air fryer
7. Bake at 200 ° C (392 ° F) for 6 minutes, turning the brioche halfway through cooking.
8. After cooking, take the brioche from the air fryer and place it on the plates.
9. Add the apples and sprinkle with powdered sugar.

2. <u>Baskets of bread, eggs, and bacon</u>

PREPARATION TIME: 15 minutes
COOKING TIME: 12 minutes
CALORIES: 327
NUTRITIONAL VALUES: CARBS: 25 GR; PROTEINS: 14 GR; FATS: 18 GR

INGREDIENTS FOR 4 SERVINGS
- 8 slices of sandwich bread
- 4 slices of bacon
- 4 eggs
- 100 gr (3.5 oz) of cheddar
- Sesame seeds to taste
- Olive oil to taste
- Salt and pepper to taste

DIRECTIONS
1. Take 4 cocottes and brush them with olive oil.
2. Put the slices of bread inside the casseroles and then line them with the bacon.
3. Add the cheddar cut into small pieces to the bottom and then peel the eggs inside each cocotte.
4. Sprinkle with pepper, salt, and sesame seeds and place the casseroles inside the air fryer.
5. Cook at 180 ° C (356 ° F) for 12 minutes.
6. After cooking, take the cocotte from the air fryer and serve.

3. <u>Cookies</u>

PREPARATION TIME: 15 minutes
COOKING TIME: 15 minutes
CALORIES: 330
NUTRITIONAL VALUES: CARBS: 55 GR; PROTEINS: 6 GR; FATS: 11 GR

INGREDIENTS FOR 4 SERVINGS
- 200 gr (7 oz) of flour
- 100 gr (3.5 oz) of butter
- 1 pinch of baking soda
- 1 egg
- 100 gr (3.5 oz) of brown sugar
- 100 gr (3.5 oz) of white sugar
- 200 gr (7 oz) of chocolate chips

- 1 pinch of salt

DIRECTIONS

1. Cut the butter into chunks, add the brown sugar and white sugar and whip them with an electric mixer.
2. Add the salt and the egg and continue whipping.
3. When the egg has been absorbed, add the baking soda and flour.
4. Stir until you get a homogeneous mixture.
5. Add the chocolate chips and mix with a spatula until they are completely incorporated.
6. Take some of the dough with a spoon and make balls with it.
7. Place a sheet of parchment paper on the bottom of the air fryer and place the balls on top.
8. Close the air fryer and cook at 180 ° C (356 ° F) for 12 minutes.
9. After cooking, take the biscuits from the air fryer, place them on a plate and let them cool before serving.

4. Croque-monsieur with salmon

PREPARATION TIME: 15 minutes
COOKING TIME: 10 minutes
CALORIES: 560
NUTRITIONAL VALUES: CARBS: 36 GR; PROTEINS: 18 GR; FATS: 11 GR

INGREDIENTS FOR 4 SERVINGS
- 250 gr (8.8 oz) of smoked salmon
- 250 gr (8.8 oz) of bechamel
- 250 gr (8.8 oz) of grilled courgettes
- 120 g (4.2 oz) of grated cheddar
- 8 slices of white bread

DIRECTIONS

1. Brush a pan with olive oil and put half the slices of bread inside.
2. Brush a little béchamel over the bread and add the zucchini, salmon, and cheddar.
3. Close with the remaining bread and then put the rest of the béchamel on top.
4. Place the baking pan in the air fryer and cook at 180 ° C (356 ° F) for 10 minutes.
5. Remove the baking pan from the air fryer, once cooked.
6. Put the croque monsieur on the plates. Serve and enjoy!

5. French toast with strawberries and fresh cheese

PREPARATION TIME: 20 minutes
COOKING TIME: 6 minutes
CALORIES: 561
NUTRITIONAL VALUES: CARBS: 24 GR; PROTEINS: 17 GR; FATS: 20 GR

INGREDIENTS FOR 4 SERVINGS

- 8 slices of brioche bread
- 2 eggs
- 60 ml (0.2 cup) of milk
- 200 gr of strawberries
- 400 gr of fresh spreadable cheese
- 2 tbsp of honey
- 1 tsp of cinnamon powder

DIRECTIONS

1. Put the fresh cheese in a bowl. Add the honey and cinnamon and mix well.
2. Wash the strawberries and cut them into thin slices.
3. Spread the cheese in half the brioche bread slices and then place the strawberries on top. Then close with the other slices of brioche bread.
4. Put the eggs in a bowl and add the milk. Mix well with a fork, and then pass the slices into the eggs.
5. Put the brioche in the air fryer and cook at 200 ° C for 6 minutes, turning the brioche after 3 minutes.
6. When the french toasts are cooked, take them out of the air fryer, put them on plates, and serve.

6. <u>Omelette with green tomatoes</u>

PREPARATION TIME: 10 minutes
COOKING TIME: 12 minutes

CALORIES: 302
NUTRITIONAL VALUES: CARBS: 6 GR; PROTEINS: 16 GR; FATS: 12 GR
INGREDIENTS FOR 4 SERVINGS

- 4 eggs
- 2 green tomatoes
- 2 minced garlic cloves
- 4 tbsp of grated Parmesan
- Dried oregano to taste
- Olive oil to taste
- Salt and pepper to taste

DIRECTIONS

1. Wash and dry the tomatoes and cut them into slices.
2. Put the tomatoes in a pan brushed with olive oil and sprinkle them with oregano, pepper, salt, and garlic.
3. Place the baking pan in the air fryer and cook at 180 ° C (356 ° F) for 5 minutes.
4. Meanwhile, break the eggs into a bowl and add Parmeasn, pepper and salt. Mix well.
5. After 4-5 minutes, pour the egg mixture over the tomatoes and continue cooking for another 7 minutes.
6. After cooking, take the baking pan from the fryer and roll the omelette on itself.
7. Cut the omelette into slices, put it on serving plates, and serve.

7. <u>Omelette with orange marmalade</u>

PREPARATION TIME: 10 minutes
COOKING TIME: 8 minutes
CALORIES: 446
NUTRITIONAL VALUES: CARBS: 31 GR; PROTEINS: 20 GR; FATS: 14 GR

INGREDIENTS FOR 4 SERVINGS

- 8 eggs
- 1 tbsp of milk
- 2 tbsp of sugar
- 4 tbsp of orange marmalade

DIRECTIONS

1. Break the eggs into a bowl and add the milk and sugar.
2. Beat them with a fork, then put them in a baking pan brushed with a little oil.
3. Place the baking pan in the air fryer and cook at 180 ° C (356 ° F) for 8 minutes.
4. After cooking, take the baking pan from the fryer and sprinkle the surface of the omelette with the jam.
5. Close the omelette into two parts, cut it into slices, divide it into serving plates and serve.

8. <u>Omelette with sausage and tomatoes</u>

PREPARATION TIME: 15 minutes
COOKING TIME: 20 minutes
CALORIES: 488
NUTRITIONAL VALUES: CARBS: 6 GR; PROTEINS: 14 GR; FATS: 16 GR

INGREDIENTS FOR 4 SERVINGS

- 6 eggs
- 3 ripe tomatoes
- 120 gr (4.2 oz) of sausage
- 1 tablespoon of chopped parsley
- Salt and pepper to taste
- Olive oil to taste

DIRECTIONS

1. Wash the tomatoes and then cut them into cubes.
2. Put the tomatoes in a baking pan and add the sausage without the casing.
3. Season with salt and pepper. Mix well and then put the baking pan in the air fryer.
4. Cook at 200 ° C (392 ° F) for 10 minutes, stirring every 2-3 minutes.
5. Meanwhile, shell the eggs in a bowl, add salt and pepper, and mix with a fork.
6. Brush another baking pan with olive oil and put the eggs inside.

7. After cooking, remove the baking pan from the air fryer and set it aside.
8. Place the eggs in the air fryer. Cook at 200 ° C (392 ° F) for 6 minutes.
9. When the eggs are cooked, take them out of the air fryer.
10. Sprinkle the eggs with the sausage and cherry tomatoes and chopped parsley
11. Close the omelette in two, cut it into slices, put it on plates, and serve.

9. Omelette with yogurt

PREPARATION TIME: 15 minutes
COOKING TIME: 10 minutes
CALORIES: 233
NUTRITIONAL VALUES: CARBS: 2 GR; PROTEINS: 18 GR; FATS: 16 GR

INGREDIENTS FOR 4 SERVINGS
- 6 eggs
- 120 gr (4.2 oz) of Greek yogurt
- 4 tbsp of flour
- 3 tbsp of chopped parsley
- Salt and pepper to taste

DIRECTIONS
1. Break the eggs into a bowl, add salt and pepper, and stir with a fork.
2. Now add the flour, yogurt and parsley and mix until you get a homogeneous mixture.

3. Brush a baking pan with olive oil and pour the egg mixture inside.
4. Place the baking pan in the air fryer and cook at 200 ° C (392 ° F) for 10 minutes.
5. After cooking, remove the omelette from the air fryer.
6. Divide the omelette into 4 parts, put it on serving plates and serve.

10. Peanut Butter Toast

PREPARATION TIME: 10 minutes
COOKING TIME: 4 minutes
CALORIES: 257
NUTRITIONAL VALUES: CARBS: 26 GR; PROTEINS: 7 GR; FATS: 11 GR

INGREDIENTS FOR 4 SERVINGS
- 4 slices of toast bread
- 4 tsp of peanut butter
- 1 apple
- Grains of pomegranate to taste

DIRECTIONS
1. Brush the basket of the air fryer with olive oil and place the slices of bread to toast at 180 ° C (356 ° F) for 2 minutes per side.
2. Meanwhile, wash the apple, remove the stem and seeds, and cut it into slices.

3. Once ready, take the bread out of the air fryer and place the slices of bread on the plates.
4. Spread the peanut butter and then put the apple slices on top.
5. Sprinkle with the pomegranate grains and serve.

11. Quatre quarts

PREPARATION TIME: 15 minutes
COOKING TIME: 30 minutes
CALORIES: 330
NUTRITIONAL VALUES: CARBS: 36 GR; PROTEINS: 4 GR; FATS: 18 GR

INGREDIENTS FOR 4 SERVINGS
- 2 medium eggs
- 80 gr (2.8 oz) of flour
- 80 gr (2.8 oz) of sugar
- 80 gr (2.8 oz) of butter
- 1 tsp of baking powder for cakes
- 1 tsp of vanilla extract
- 1 pinch of salt
- Powdered sugar to taste

DIRECTIONS
1. Melt the butter and let it cool.
2. Meanwhile, put the eggs, sugar and vanilla in a bowl.
3. Beat the eggs with an electric mixer. Add the yeast, salt, and flour when you get a light and soft mixture.
4. Mix well, and finally, add the melted butter.

5. Stir until you get a homogeneous and lump-free mixture and then pour it into a pound cake mold brushed with olive oil.
6. Place the mold in the air fryer and cook at 200 ° C (392 ° F) for 25 minutes.
7. After cooking, remove the mold from the air fryer and let the cake cool completely.
8. When it is cold, pour the Quatre Quarts into a serving dish for desserts.
9. Sprinkle the cake with icing sugar, cut it into slices and serve.

12. Spinach, bacon, and cheddar omelette

PREPARATION TIME: 10 minutes
COOKING TIME: 10 minutes
CALORIES: 549
NUTRITIONAL VALUES: CARBS: 3 GR; PROTEINS: 11 GR; FATS: 15 GR

INGREDIENTS FOR 4 SERVINGS
- 8 eggs
- 150 gr (5.2 oz) of boiled spinach
- 100 gr (3.5 oz) of smoked bacon
- 150 gr (5.2 oz) of cheddar
- Olive oil to taste
- Salt and pepper to taste

DIRECTIONS

1. Cut the bacon into cubes. Brush a baking pan with olive oil and put the bacon and the spinach inside.
2. Put the baking pan in the air fryer.
3. Cook at 180 ° C (356 ° F) for 3 minutes.
4. Meanwhile, break the eggs into a bowl, add salt and pepper and the diced cheddar, and mix well with a fork.
5. After 3 minutes, pour the egg mixture over the spinach and bacon and continue cooking for another 7 minutes.
6. After cooking, take the baking pan from the fryer and fold the omelette into two parts.
7. Cut the omelette into slices, place them on serving plates and serve.

13.   Toast with avocado and bacon

PREPARATION TIME: 15 minutes
COOKING TIME: 4 minutes
CALORIES: 580
NUTRITIONAL VALUES: CARBS: 43 GR; PROTEINS: 12 GR; FATS: 16 GR

INGREDIENTS FOR 4 SERVINGS

- 8 slices of toast bread
- 1 ripe avocado
- 100 gr (3.5 oz) of bacon
- Balsamic vinegar to taste

DIRECTIONS

1. Peel the avocado and remove the core. Cut the pulp into thin slices.
2. Put the avocado on top of half of the slices of toast and then put the bacon on top.
3. Sprinkle with balsamic vinegar and close with the other half of the bread.
4. Brush the air fryer basket with olive oil and place the toast inside.
5. Bake at 200 ° C (392 ° F) for 4 minutes, turning the toasts halfway through cooking.
6. Once cooked, take the toasts from the air fryer, and place them on the plates.
7. Cut the toast into two triangles and serve.

14.   Toast with tuna and fresh cheese

PREPARATION TIME: 15 minutes
COOKING TIME: 4 minutes
CALORIES: 336
NUTRITIONAL VALUES: CARBS: 27 GR; PROTEINS: 16 GR; FATS: 18 GR

INGREDIENTS FOR 4 SERVINGS

- 100 gr (3.5 oz) of drained tuna in oil
- 140 gr (4.9 oz) of fresh spreadable cheese
- 8 slices of bread for sandwiches
- 1 red onion

- 100 gr (3.5 oz) cherry tomatoes 100 g
- Dried oregano to taste
- Olive oil to taste

DIRECTIONS

1. Wash the cherry tomatoes and cut them into slices.
2. Peel the onion and cut it into slices.
3. Spread half of the slices of bread with fresh cheese and then put the cherry tomatoes and onion on top.
4. Add the tuna and sprinkle with dried oregano.
5. Close the toast with the other half of the bread and place them in the basket of the air fryer brushed with olive oil.
6. Bake at 200 ° C (392 ° F) for 4 minutes, turning the bread after 2 minutes.
7. When the toasts are cooked, put them on serving plates, cut them into two triangles, and serve.

15. <u>Welsh cakes</u>

PREPARATION TIME: 20 minutes
COOKING TIME: 16 minutes
CALORIES: 431
NUTRITIONAL VALUES: CARBS: 59 GR; PROTEINS: 6 GR; FATS: 16 GR

INGREDIENTS FOR 4 SERVINGS

- 135 gr (4.7 oz) of flour
- 55 gr (1.9 oz) of cold butter
- 1 tsp of baking powder
- 20 gr (0.7 oz) of raisins
- 45 grams (1.5 oz) of granulated sugar
- brown sugar
- 1 egg
- 1 pinch of salt

DIRECTIONS

1. Put the flour, baking powder, sugar, salt and then butter (cut into cubes) in a bowl.
2. Take an electric mixer and work the ingredients at low speed.
3. Now add the egg and raisins and mix well.
4. Now knead the mixture with your hands, until you get a dough with a consistency similar to the shortcrust pastry.
5. Form a loaf and roll it out with a rolling pin on a a floured table.
6. With a pastry cutter of about 6 cm, form many dough discs.
7. Brush the basket of the air fryer and put the dough discs inside.
8. Cook at 200 ° C (392 ° F) for 3 minutes per side.
9. Put some brown sugar on a plate and, when the Welsh cakes are cooked, pass them over the sugar on both sides.
10. Now put the Welsh cakes on the serving plates and serve.

Appetizer and snack

Appetizer

16. Fried cod bites

PREPARATION TIME: 15 minutes
COOKING TIME: 12 minutes
CALORIES: 414
NUTRITIONAL VALUES: CARBS: 20 GR; PROTEINS: 31 GR; FATS: 12 GR

INGREDIENTS FOR 4 SERVINGS
- 800 gr of cod fillet
- Flour to taste
- Salt and pepper to taste
- Olive oil to taste

DIRECTIONS
1. Remove the fish bones and skin, wash them, and cut them into cubes.

2. Put the cod cubes in a bowl and add salt, pepper, and flour.
3. Stir until the cod is completely floured.
4. Put the cod cubes in the air fryer, adding a bit of oil on the surface.
5. Close the air fryer and cook at 180 ° C (356 ° F) for 12 minutes, stirring the fish every 3 minutes and sprinkling more oil if necessary.
6. Once cooked, take the cod from the fryer, put it on serving plates, and serve.

17. Gratin oysters

PREPARATION TIME: 15 minutes
COOKING TIME: 10 minutes
CALORIES: 279
NUTRITIONAL VALUES: CARBS: 17 GR; PROTEINS: 18 GR; FATS: 15 GR

INGREDIENTS FOR 4 SERVINGS
- 16 oysters already opened and cleaned
- 100 g (3.5 oz) of breadcrumbs
- 6 chopped mint leaves
- 4 cherry tomatoes
- Salt and pepper to taste
- Olive oil to taste

DIRECTIONS
1. Wash the cherry tomatoes and cut them into cubes.

2. Put the cherry tomatoes in a bowl and add the breadcrumbs, mint, salt, pepper and 4 tablespoons of olive oil. Mix until you get a homogeneous breading.
3. Place the oysters in the air fryer and cover them with the breading.
4. Close the air fryer and cook at 180 ° C (356 ° F) for 10 minutes.
5. Once cooked, take the oysters from the air fryer, place them on serving plates, and serve.

18. Leek mini quiches

PREPARATION TIME: 15 minutes
COOKING TIME: 25 minutes
CALORIES: 368
NUTRITIONAL VALUES: CARBS: 26 GR; PROTEINS: 13 GR; FATS: 24 GR

INGREDIENTS FOR 4 SERVINGS
- 1 roll of puff pastry
- 20 gr (0.7 oz) of cheddar
- 2 leeks
- 2 whole eggs
- 200 gr (7 oz) of cooking cream
- Nutmeg to taste
- Salt and pepper to taste

DIRECTIONS
1. Remove the hardest part from the leeks, wash them, and cut them into rings.

2. Place the leeks in the air fryer, season with oil, salt and pepper, and cook at 180 ° C (356 ° F) for 5 minutes.
3. After 5 minutes, take the leeks from the fryer and put them in a bowl.
4. Add the eggs, cooking cream, chopped cheddar and nutmeg and mix well.
5. Roll out the puff pastry. Cut it into small discs of dough.
6. Brush canapes molds with olive oil and put the puff pastry inside.
7. Put the leek mixture on the bottom and put the molds in the air fryer.
8. Cook at 200 ° C (392 ° F) for 20 minutes.
9. After cooking, take the mini quiche out of the air fryer and let them cool.
10. When the quiches have cooled, remove them from the molds, place them on plates and serve.

19. <u>Prawns with green pepper</u>

PREPARATION TIME: 10 minutes
COOKING TIME: 10 minutes
CALORIES: 220
NUTRITIONAL VALUES: CARBS: 3 GR; PROTEINS: 16 GR; FATS: 8 GR

INGREDIENTS FOR 4 SERVINGS
- 8 king prawns
- 2 tsp of green peppercorns
- 1 tbsp of chopped parsley
- ½ glass of white wine
- Olive oil to taste
- Salt and pepper to taste

DIRECTIONS
1. Put salt, pepper, wine, parsley and 2 tablespoons of olive oil in a bowl and mix well.
2. Remove the prawn heads, wash them, and put them in the bowl with the emulsion.
3. Mix well, and then put the prawns in a baking pan.
4. Add the green peppercorns and put the baking pan inside the air fryer.
5. Cook at 180 ° C (356 ° F for 10 minutes)
6. Once cooked, take the prawns from the air fryer, place them on plates, and serve.

20. <u>Quiche asparagus and bacon</u>

PREPARATION TIME: 20 minutes
COOKING TIME: 20 minutes
CALORIES: 617
NUTRITIONAL VALUES: CARBS: 31 GR; PROTEINS: 23 GR; FATS: 34 GR

INGREDIENTS FOR 4 SERVINGS
- 1 roll of puff pastry

- 200 gr (7 oz) of fresh spreadable cheese
- 300 gr (10.5 oz) of cooked asparagus
- 60 gr (2.1 oz) of bacon
- 3 tbsp of grated Parmesan cheese
- 2 eggs
- 1 shallot
- Salt and pepper to taste

DIRECTIONS
1. Peel and chop the shallot.
2. Put the fresh spreadable cheese in a bowl and add the eggs.
3. Mix well and add the Parmesan, salt, pepper, shallot, diced bacon, and chopped asparagus.
4. Brush a round mold with olive oil and line it with the puff pastry.
5. Fill the puff pastry and place the mold in the air fryer.
6. Cook at 180 ° C (355 ° F) for 20 minutes.
7. When the quiche is cooked, remove it from the air fryer and let it cool.
8. When the quiche is cold, cut it into slices, put it on plates, and serve.

21. **Salmon and dill tartlets**

PREPARATION TIME: 15 minutes
COOKING TIME: 15 minutes
CALORIES: 390

NUTRITIONAL VALUES: CARBS: 29 GR; PROTEINS: 20 GR; FATS: 13 GR

INGREDIENTS FOR 4 SERVINGS
- 1 roll of puff pastry
- 300 gr (10.5 oz) of smoked salmon
- 100 g (3.5 oz) of Greek yogurt
- 2 sprigs of dill
- 1 lemon
- Chopped chives to taste
- Salt and pepper to taste

DIRECTIONS
1. Wash the dill, chop it, and put it in a bowl.
2. Chop the salmon and put it in the bowl with the dill.
3. Add the grated lemon zest, pepper, salt, and Greek yogurt and mix well.
4. Roll out the puff pastry and cut it into 4 circles.
5. Brush 4 tartlet molds with olive oil and put the puff pastry inside.
6. Fill the tartlets with the salmon filling and place the molds in the air fryer.
7. Cook at 180 ° C (356 ° F) for 15 minutes.
8. When the tartlets are cooked, remove them from the air fryer and let them cool.
9. Once cold, remove the tartlets from the molds, place them on serving plates, sprinkle them with chopped chives and serve.

22. Shrimp skewers with lime, honey, and sesame seeds

PREPARATION TIME: 15 minutes
COOKING TIME: 8 minutes
CALORIES: 396
NUTRITIONAL VALUES: CARBS: 16 GR; PROTEINS: 51 GR; FATS: 11 GR

INGREDIENTS FOR 4 SERVINGS

- 6 limes
- 2 tsp of toasted sesame seeds
- ½ glass of white wine
- 800 gr (28.2 oz) of shrimps
- Salt and pepper to taste
- Olive oil to taste

DIRECTIONS

1. Shell the shrimps, wash them and dry them with a paper towel.
2. Wash 4 limes and cut them into rings.
3. Squeeze the other two limes into a bowl, add the wine, oil, salt and pepper, and mix.
4. Start forming the skewers. First, put a slice of lime and then a shrimp. Proceed until the end of all the ingredients.
5. Brush the skewers with the emulsion and put them in the air fryer.
6. Cook the skewers at 180 ° C (356 ° F) for 8 minutes, turning them halfway through cooking and brushing them with the emulsion.
7. Once cooked, take the shrimp and lime skewers from the fryer, and place them on serving plates.
8. Sprinkle the skewers with toasted sesame seeds. Serve and enjoy!

23. Shrimp with cornflakes

PREPARATION TIME: 20 minutes
COOKING TIME: 10 minutes
CALORIES: 408
NUTRITIONAL VALUES: CARBS: 12 GR; PROTEINS: 24 GR; FATS: 11 GR

INGREDIENTS FOR 4 SERVINGS

- 800 gr (28.2 oz) of shrimps
- 1 lemon
- Cornflakes to taste
- 1 tbsp of chopped chives
- Salt and pepper to taste
- Olive oil to taste

DIRECTIONS

1. Shell the shrimps, wash them and then dry them.
2. Put 4 tablespoons of olive oil, salt, pepper, lemon juice and chives in a bowl and mix well.
3. Put the shrimps in the bowl with the marinade. Let it rest for 12-14 minutes.

4. Meanwhile, crumble the cornflakes and place them in a bowl.
5. After 15 minutes, put the shrimps in the bowl with the cornflakes and stir until completely covered.
6. Put the shrimps inside the air fryer, sprinkle a little oil, close, and cook at 180 ° C (356 ° F) for 10 minutes, shaking the basket every 3 minutes.
7. Once cooked, take the shrimps from the fryer, put them on the plates, and serve.

Snacks

24. **Bacon and peppers biscuits**

PREPARATION TIME: 20 minutes
COOKING TIME: 12 minutes
CALORIES: 235
NUTRITIONAL VALUES: CARBS: 38 GR; PROTEINS: 9 GR; FATS: 12 GR

INGREDIENTS FOR 4 SERVINGS
- 100 gr (3.5 oz) of flour
- 1 small red pepper
- 50 gr (1.7 oz) of softened butter
- 80 gr of grated Parmesan cheese
- 8 slices of bacon
- Salt and pepper to taste

DIRECTIONS
1. Cut the butter into chunks and put it in a bowl.
2. Add the Parmesan and flour and mix well until you get a homogeneous mixture.
3. Wash the pepper and remove the seeds. Cut it into small pieces.
4. Also, cut the bacon into small pieces.
5. Put the pepper, bacon, salt, and pepper into the dough and knead until all the ingredients are well incorporated.
6. Cover the bowl with the dough and let it rest for 15 minutes.
7. After, roll out the dough on a lightly floured surface and form many biscuits.
8. Place the biscuits inside the air fryer and cook at 180 ° C (356 ° F) for 12 minutes.
9. Once cooked, take the biscuits from the air fryer, place them on a serving dish, let them cool and then serve.

25. **Baskets of asparagus and ham**

PREPARATION TIME: 15 minutes
COOKING TIME: 20 minutes
CALORIES: 264
NUTRITIONAL VALUES: CARBS: 30 GR; PROTEINS: 12 GR; FATS: 12 GR

INGREDIENTS FOR 4 SERVINGS

- 400 gr (14 oz) of asparagus
- 1 roll of puff pastry
- 12 slices of ham
- 100 gr (3.5 oz) of cheddar
- 1 minced clove of garlic
- Salt and pepper to taste
- Olive oil to taste

DIRECTIONS

1. Wash the asparagus and cut them into small pieces.
2. Heat a little oil in a pan, sauté the garlic for 2 minutes and then add the asparagus.
3. Cook for 4 minutes, season with salt and pepper and then turn off.
4. Take the puff pastry, roll it out on a floured table and cut it into 6 squares.
5. Put the puff pastry inside 6 muffin molds brushed with olive oil.
6. Place two slices of ham, the asparagus, and finally, the diced cheddar.
7. Place the molds inside the air fryer and cook at 200 ° C (392 ° F) for 16 minutes.
8. After cooking, remove the muffin molds from the air fryer and let them rest for 2-3 minutes.
9. Remove the asparagus and han baskets from the molds and place them on plates. Serve and enjoy!

26. <u>Baskets of bread</u>

PREPARATION TIME: 10 minutes
COOKING TIME: 10 minutes
CALORIES: 412
NUTRITIONAL VALUES: CARBS: 40 GR; PROTEINS: 7 GR; FATS: 10 GR
INGREDIENTS FOR 4 SERVINGS

- 8 slices of sandwich bread
- 60 g (2.1 oz) of grated cheese
- 6 tbsp of tomato sauce
- 4 tbsp of olive oil
- Dried oregano to taste
- Salt and pepper to taste

DIRECTIONS

1. Brush muffin molds with olive oil and place the slices of bread inside.
2. Fill the bread with oil, tomato sauce, cheese, salt and pepper, and sprinkle with dried oregano.
3. Place the molds in the air fryer and cook at 180 ° C (356 ° F) for 10 minutes.
4. After cooking, remove the molds from the air fryer and let them cool for a few minutes.
5. Remove the bread baskets from the molds, place them on the plates and serve.

27. <u>Muffins with zucchini and cheese</u>

PREPARATION TIME: 15 minutes
COOKING TIME: 22 minutes
CALORIES: 300
NUTRITIONAL VALUES: CARBS: 30 GR; PROTEINS: 14 GR; FATS: 12 GR
INGREDIENTS FOR 4 SERVINGS

- 150 gr (5.2 oz) of flour
- 120 ml (1/2 cup) of milk
- 30 g (1 oz) of grated Parmesan cheese
- 1 egg
- 2 tsp of baking powder
- 150 gr (5.2 oz) of zucchinis
- 100 gr (3.5 oz) of cheddar
- 10 pitted black olives
- Salt and pepper to taste
- 3 tbsp of olive oil

DIRECTIONS

1. Wash the zucchini, grate them, and put them in a bowl.
2. Break the egg into another bowl. Add all the oil. Beat them with a whisk until they are completely blended.
3. Pour in the milk and mix again.
4. Now add the flour, salt, and baking powder. Mix everything together.
5. Add the grated Parmesan, chopped olives and diced cheddar.
6. Mix well, and finally, add the zucchini.

7. Brush muffin molds with olive oil and put the dough inside.
8. Place the molds in the air fryer and cook at 180 ° C (356 ° F) for 22 minutes.
9. When the muffins are cooked, remove them from the air fryer and let them cool.
10. Once cooled, remove the muffins from the molds, and you can serve.

28. <u>Potato pancakes</u>

PREPARATION TIME: 15 minutes
COOKING TIME: 10 minutes
CALORIES: 75
NUTRITIONAL VALUES: CARBS: 12 GR; PROTEINS: 1 GR; FATS: 6 GR

INGREDIENTS FOR 4 SERVINGS

- 4 large, boiled potatoes
- 2 tbsp of flour
- 2 sprigs of rosemary
- Salt and pepper to taste
- Olive oil to taste

DIRECTIONS

1. Peel the potatoes and mash them with a potato masher in a bowl.
2. Wash the rosemary, chop the needles, and put them in the bowl with the potatoes.
3. Add some oil and mix well.
4. Now add the flour, pepper and salt. Mix well.

5. Form 20 meatballs with your hands and then mash them.
6. Brush the bottom of the air fryer with olive oil and put the potato pancakes inside.
7. Sprinkle a little oil on the surface and cook at 200 ° C (392 ° F) for 10 minutes, turning the pancakes after 5 minutes.
8. When the pancakes are cooked, take them out of the air fryer, place them on serving plates and serve.

29. <u>Pretzels with salmon</u>

PREPARATION TIME: 15 minutes
COOKING TIME: 15 minutes
CALORIES: 337
NUTRITIONAL VALUES: CARBS: 27 GR; PROTEINS: 18 GR; FATS: 23 GR

INGREDIENTS FOR 4 SERVINGS
- 2 rolls of puff pastry
- 200 gr (7 oz) of fresh spreadable cheese
- 180 gr (6.3 oz) of smoked salmon
- 1 egg
- 2 tbsp of milk
- Black sesame seeds to taste

DIRECTIONS
1. Roll out a sheet of puff pastry and spread the cheese over the entire surface.
2. Add the smoked salmon and close it with the other puff pastry roll.
3. Seal the edges well and brush the surface with beaten egg together with the milk.
4. Sprinkle the surface of the puff pastry with the sesame seeds and then, with a pasta cutter, cut the dough into many small squares.
5. Brush the air fryer basket with olive oil and put the pretzels inside.
6. Cook at 180 ° C (356 ° F) for 15 minutes, shaking the basket from time to time.
7. After cooking, take the pretzels from the air fryer and place them in a serving dish.
8. Let the pretzels cool, and then serve.

30. <u>Savory shortbreads</u>

PREPARATION TIME: 15 minutes
COOKING TIME: 12 minutes
CALORIES: 240
NUTRITIONAL VALUES: CARBS: 18 GR; PROTEINS: 3 GR; FATS: 15 GR

INGREDIENTS FOR 4 SERVINGS
- 150 gr (5.2 oz) of flour
- 100 gr (3.5 oz) of cold butter

- 4 tbsp of grated Parmesan cheese
- 1 small egg yolk
- 10 basil leaves
- 4 sage leaves
- 1 tsp of paprika
- Salt and pepper to taste

DIRECTIONS

1. Wash and dry the sage and basil and then chop them.
2. Put the flour, the butter (cut into chunks), the egg, and the Parmesan in a bowl.
3. Knead with your hands until you get a sandy mixture.
4. Add sage and basil and continue kneading.
5. Finally, add the paprika, salt and pepper, and finish kneading.
6. Form a sausage with the sides in a cylinder and wrap it in cling film. Let it rest in the freezer for 10 minutes.
7. After 10 minutes, take the dough and cut it into slices.
8. Score the surface of the biscuits with the tines of a fork.
9. Brush the air fryer basket with olive oil and place your biscuits inside.
10. Cook at 180 ° C (356 ° F) for 12 minutes.
11. Once cooked, take the biscuits from the air fryer, place them on a serving dish, let them cool and then serve.

Poultry and turkey

Poultry

31. <u>Cranberry and oranges Guinea fowl</u>

PREPARATION TIME: 10 minutes
COOKING TIME: 30 minutes
CALORIES: 490
NUTRITIONAL VALUES: CARBS; 14 GR; PROTEINS: 32 GR; FATS: 20 GR

INGREDIENTS FOR 4 SERVINGS

- 1 guinea fowl cut into pieces of 1 kg (2.2 lbs)
- 1 blood orange
- 1 stalk of celery
- 1 carrot
- 200 grams (7 oz) of cranberries
- 40 grams (3 tbsp) of butter
- 2 tbsp of brown sugar
- Olive oil to taste
- Salt and pepper to taste

DIRECTIONS

1. Firs, peel the carrot and then chop it.
2. Wash the celery and then chop it.
3. Wash and dry the guinea fowl, then place it in a pan brushed with olive oil.
4. Add the celery and carrot, season with oil, salt and pepper, and the blood orange juice.
5. Place the pan inside the fryer and cook at 200°C (392°F) for about 30 minutes (always check the cooking).
6. Meanwhile, wash the cranberries.
7. Melt the butter and then add the cranberries.
8. Stir, add sugar, and cook for 5 minutes.
9. When cooked, turn off and blend the cranberries with an immersion blender.
10. When the guinea fowl is cooked, remove the pan from the fryer and let it rest for 2 minutes.
11. Now put the guinea fowl on the serving plates.
12. Sprinkle with the cranberry sauce and serve.

32. Jalapeno and sage chicken legs

PREPARATION TIME: 5 minutes
COOKING TIME: 25 minutes
CALORIES: 230
NUTRITIONAL VALUES: CARBS: 4 GR; PROTEINS: 28 GR; FATS: 11 GR

INGREDIENTS FOR 4 SERVINGS

- 8 chicken legs
- 2 tsp of chopped jalapeno
- Breadcrumbs to taste
- 1 tbsp of chopped sage
- Olive oil to taste
- Salt to taste

DIRECTIONS

1. Firs, put the breadcrumbs, salt, chopped jalapeno and sage in a bowl.
2. Mix everything evenly.
3. Brush or scrub the chicken legs with very little oil.
4. Dip the chicken legs in the flavored breadcrumbs.
5. Preheat the air fryer to 200 ° C (392°F).
6. Place the chicken legs inside.
7. Cook for 15 minutes at this temperature, then for 10 minutes at a lower temperature (170 °C - 338°F). Check the cooking and, if they are ready, remove the chicken legs from the air fryer.
8. Serve the chicken legs still warm.

33. Mushroom tomato and ham chicken

PREPARATION TIME: 10 minutes
COOKING TIME: 15 minutes
CALORIES: 320
NUTRITIONAL VALUES: CARBS: 10 GR; PROTEINS: 32 GR; FATS: 6 GR

INGREDIENTS FOR 4 SERVINGS

- 700 grams (24.6 oz) of chicken breast
- 2 tbsp of all-purpose flour
- 15 ml (1 tbsp and 1 tsp) of olive oil
- 400 grams (2 cups) of button mushrooms
- 4 slices of cooked ham
- 200 grams (1 cup) of tomatoes
- 1 garlic clove
- dried oregano to taste

DIRECTIONS

1. First, lightly remove the soil and rub from button mushrooms with a damp cloth. Cut them into slices and put them on a plate.
2. Peel and mince garlic clove.
3. Put the flour on a plate and flour the chicken breasts.
4. Preheat the air fryer to 200 ºC (392ºF) for a few minutes.
5. Place the slices of meat sprinkled with a bit of oil, mushrooms, minced garlic, and the ham cut into small pieces into the basket.
6. Wash the tomatoes, cut them in half, and add them to the rest of the ingredients with the mushrooms.
7. Cook for 15 minutes. The meat will become golden brown.
8. Serve the chicken slices with the rest of the ingredients, still hot.

34. Olives and pecans chicken

PREPARATION TIME: 10 minutes
COOKING TIME: 12/15 minutes
CALORIES: 340
NUTRITIONAL VALUES: CARBS: 14 GR; PROTEIN: 30 GR; FATS: 12 GR

INGREDIENTS FOR 4 SERVINGS

- 600 gr (21.1 oz) of chicken breast
- 16 black olives
- 3 tbsp of chopped pecans
- 1 teaspoon Olive oil
- 100 gr (3.5 oz) of Breadcrumbs
- 2 tbsp of grated Parmesan cheese
- 1 tbsp chopped aromatic herbs (thyme, rosemary, oregano, parsley, basil)
- Salt to taste.

DIRECTIONS

1. First, clean and cut the chicken breast into chunks or strips.

2. Put the chicken in a bowl with the black olives, season with a single teaspoon of oil and mix.
3. Mix the breadcrumbs, pecans, Parmesan, salt and chopped aromatic herbs. Add the chicken to the breadcrumbs and mix so that it adheres perfectly.
4. Distribute the chicken and olives directly to the previously oiled basket of the fryer.
5. Cook the chicken at 200 ° C (392°F) for 12/15 minutes, turning them gently halfway through cooking.
6. Depending on the size of the morsels, the minutes may also vary (some less or more).
7. Always check for cooking.
8. Serve the pecan-breaded chicken and olive still hot.

35. <u>Spinach and cheddar chicken nuggets</u>

PREPARATION TIME: 10 minutes
COOKING TIME: 20 minutes
CALORIES: 310
NUTRITIONAL VALUES: CARBS: 10 GR; PROTEIN: 30 GR; FATS: 7 GR

INGREDIENTS FOR 4 SERVINGS
- 500 gr chicken breast (17.5 oz)
- 200 gr (1 cup) of spinach (already boiled and drained)
- 60 gr (1/4 cup) of grated cheddar cheese
- 2 big eggs
- Olive oil to taste
- Breadcrumbs to taste
- Salt to taste

DIRECTIONS
1. First, boil the cleaned and sliced chicken breast in a pan or saucepan, covering it with water.
2. Add salt and finish cooking.
3. Boil the spinach or let it defrost if you are using frozen ones.
4. Let them drain well: this step is very important to prevent the dough from being too watery and soft.
5. Blend the spinach and then the chicken in a blender, reducing them to puree.
6. Combine the spinach, chicken, eggs, cheddar and salt in a bowl.
7. Stir with a spoon until all the ingredients are combined, and the mixture is soft and compact.
8. Shape into nuggets by dividing the dough into equal parts and pressing them so that they take shape.
9. After forming the spinach, pass them into the breadcrumbs.
10. Place them and sprinkle them with olive oil on the air fryer previously heated to 200 ° C (392°F) and cook

for about 10 minutes, turning them halfway through cooking, until golden brown.

11. Serve still hot.

36. **Vinegar and chili sauce chicken wings**

PREPARATION TIME: 10 minutes
COOKING TIME: 20 minutes
CALORIES: 320
NUTRITIONAL VALUES: CARBS: 10 GR; PROTEIN: 28 GR; FATS: 8 GR

INGREDIENTS FOR 4 SERVINGS

- 12 chicken wings
- 4 tbsp of all-purpose flour
- 1 sprig of chopped parsley
- 1 shallot
- 3 tbsp of apple cider vinegar
- 1 tbsp of chopped red chili pepper
- Olive oil
- Salt and pepper to taste

DIRECTIONS

1. First, cut the chicken wings in half and remove the tip. Wash them and then pat them with a paper towel.
2. Add a pinch of salt and pepper.
3. Put the all-purpose flour on a plate and then flour the wings on both sides.
4. Put the wings in the air fryer and sprinkle them with olive oil. Cook at

180°C (356°F) for 18-20 minutes, turning them after 10 minutes.

5. Meanwhile, prepare the sauce.
6. Peel the shallot, cut into pieces, and put it in the blender glass.
7. Add 3 tbsp of oil, parsley, vinegar, chopped chili pepper, salt and pepper.
8. Blend on high speed until you get a dense and homogeneous sauce.
9. When cooked, remove the wings from the fryer and place them on the plates.
10. Sprinkle with the vinegar sauce and serve.

37. **Zucchini and sweet potato chicken**

PREPARATION TIME: 10 minutes
COOKING TIME: 15 minutes
CALORIES: 380
NUTRITIONAL VALUES: CARBS: 18 GR; PROTEINS: 36 GR; FATS: 8 GR

INGREDIENTS FOR 4 SERVINGS

- 800 grams (4 cups) of chicken breast
- 2 zucchinis
- 4 sweet Potatoes
- 2 tbsp of breadcrumbs
- 2 tbsp of Parmesan cheese
- 2 tsp of olive oil
- Salt to taste

DIRECTIONS

1. First, you can wash and peel the 2 zucchinis, cutting them into very thin slices.
2. Peel the sweet potatoes, wash them, and cut them into a crescent.
3. At the same time, prepare the breading: mix the breadcrumbs and Parmesan in a dish.
4. Put the chicken, zucchinis and sweet potatoes in a large bowl and add the breadcrumbs and Parmesan topping.
5. Stir to distribute evenly.
6. Then put all the ingredients directly on the air fryer's basket (or in a suitable baking pan).
7. Sprinkle or grease with a bit of olive oil.
8. Cook the ingredients at 200°C (392°F) in the air fryer for 12/15 minutes. Turn them and check that they are cooked and golden, otherwise, continue for another 2-3 minutes.
9. Serve hot.

Turkey

38. <u>Bell peppers and basil turkey rolls</u>

PREPARATION TIME: 10 minutes
COOKING TIME: 15 minutes

CALORIES: 320
NUTRITIONAL VALUES: CARBS: 12 GR; PROTEINS: 28 GR; FATS: 3 GR

INGREDIENTS FOR 4 SERVINGS

- 4 big turkey slices
- 2 red bell peppers
- 1 shallot
- 1 glass of white wine (200 ml)
- 1 tsp of chopped basil
- Olive oil to taste
- Salt and pepper to taste

DIRECTIONS

1. First, peel the shallot and then cut it into thin slices.
2. Remove the cap, the seeds, and the white filaments from the peppers. Wash red bell peppers and cut them into slices.
3. Remove the excess fat from the turkey slices.
4. Put a bit of oil in a pan, let it heat up and then add the shallot.
5. Sauté for 2 minutes, add the peppers and cook for 5 minutes.
6. Add a pinch of salt and pepper. Turn off, sprinkle with basil, and mix well.
7. Season the turkey slices with pepper and salt and put the peppers inside the meat.
8. Roll the slices on themselves and keep them closed with a toothpick.
9. Brush the meat with oil and white wine and place it inside the air fryer.

10. Cook at 200 °C (392°F) for 10 minutes, turning the rolls after 5 minutes.
11. Once cooked, remove the turkey rolls from the air fryer.
12. Put them on plates, remove the toothpicks and serve.

39. Blue cheese sauce rosemary turkey

PREPARATION TIME: 15 minutes
COOKING TIME: 15 minutes
CALORIES: 430
NUTRITIONAL VALUES: CARBS: 2 GR; PROTEINS: 38 GR; FATS: 14 GR

INGREDIENTS FOR 4 SERVINGS

- 600 gr (21.1 oz) of turkey breast in one piece
- 8 slices of ham
- 1 sprig of rosemary
- 100 ml (1 cup) of half and half
- 100 grams (3.5 oz) of blue cheese
- Olive oil to taste
- Salt and pepper to taste

DIRECTIONS

1. Wash and dry the turkey breast and then massage the entire surface of the meat with salt and pepper.
2. Cut the turkey into 4 slices of the same size.
3. Wrap the turkey with the slices of ham and then tie the meat with kitchen string.
4. Wash the sprig of rosemary and divide it into four parts.
5. Put the rosemary between the kitchen string and the turkey meat.
6. Brush the meat with olive oil and then place it in the air fryer basket.
7. If your deep fryer is not big enough, you can cook the fillet in two separate cooks.
8. Cook the fillets at 200°C (392°F) for 6 minutes, then turn the slices. Cook for another 6 minutes.
9. When cooked, remove them from the fryer and wrap them in aluminum foil.
10. Then proceed to prepare the accompanying sauce.
11. Cut the blue cheese into cubes and put it in a saucepan with half and half.
12. Put the saucepan on the stove; cook until the cheese has entirely melted and the sauce has taken on a thick and homogeneous consistency.
13. Remove the turkey breast from the aluminum foil and free it from the kitchen string.
14. Put the turkey slices on serving plates, sprinkle them with the blue cheese sauce and serve.

40. Brandy and raw ham turkey

PREPARATION TIME: 10 minutes
COOKING TIME: 20 minutes
CALORIES: 350
NUTRITIONAL VALUES: CARBS: 3 GR; PROTEINS: 32 GR; FATS: 14 GR

INGREDIENTS FOR 4 SERVINGS

- 4 turkey breasts pieces (600 grams or 18 oz)
- 60 gr (or ¼ cup) of coarsely chopped raw ham
- 30 gr (or 2 tbsp) of dried mushrooms softened in warm water
- 2 sage leaves
- 2 tbsp of brandy
- 100 grams (1 cup) of butter
- 2 tablespoons of all-purpose flour
- Salt and pepper to taste

DIRECTIONS

1. First, you should wash the turkey breasts, dry them, and lightly flour them.
2. Make them in a suitable air fryer pan with half the cut butter and the washed sage leaves.
3. Add the brandy too. Let it marinate for 10 minutes.
4. Squeeze and chop the mushrooms.
5. Now distribute over the turkey breast the mixture of mushrooms and raw ham.
6. Arrange the turkey in the preheated air fryer at 200° C (392°F) for 15/20 minutes.
7. Serve the turkey breasts still hot.

41. Hot spicy turkey

PREPARATION TIME: 5 minutes
COOKING TIME: 25 minutes
CALORIES: 280
NUTRITIONAL VALUES: CARBS: 1 GR; PROTEINS: 30 GR; FATS: 1 GR

INGREDIENTS FOR 4 SERVINGS

- 600 gr (3 cups) of turkey breast
- 1 tbsp of spice mix
- 1 tbsp of Tabasco sauce
- Salt and pepper to taste

DIRECTIONS

1. First, wash and dry the turkey breast.
2. Put the turkey in a bowl to marinate with the mixed spicy seasoning and Tabasco sauce for at least 30 minutes.
3. Once the turkey breast has been marinated, remove it from the marinade and place it in the air fryer's basket (or a suitable baking pan).
4. Cook the chicken turkey for about 20/25 minutes with the air fryer set at 180°C (338°F).

5. Halfway through cooking, turn the hot turkey, shaking the air fryer's basket.
6. Serve the hot spicy turkey immediately.

42. Nuts, sage and bacon turkey rolls

PREPARATION TIME: 5 minutes
COOKING TIME: 10 minutes
CALORIES: 420
NUTRITIONAL VALUES: CARBS: 12 GR; PROTEINS: 35 GR; FATS: 16 GR

INGREDIENTS FOR 4 SERVINGS

- 8 slices of turkey breast (770 grams or 1.7 lbs)
- 8 thin slices of bacon
- 1 cup (100 grams) of mixed chopped nuts
- 4 sage leaves
- Olive oil to taste
- Salt and pepper to taste

DIRECTIONS

1. Wash the turkey meat and dry it with a paper towel.
2. Wash and dry the sage leaves and then chop them.
3. Add salt and pepper on both sides of the turkey slice.
4. Place a slice of bacon and little chopped nuts inside each slice.
5. Add the sage and then roll the slices on themselves.
6. Keep the slices closed with a toothpick.
7. Brush the meat with olive oil and place it inside the air fryer.
8. Cook at 200 °C (392°F) for 10 minutes.
9. Once cooked, remove the turkey from the air fryer and place it on serving plates.
10. Remove the toothpick and serve.

43. Salami and peas turkey meatloaf

PREPARATION TIME: 10 minutes
COOKING TIME: 25 minutes
CALORIES: 420
NUTRITIONAL VALUES: CARBS: 13 GR; PROTEINS: 32 GR; FATS: 16 GR

INGREDIENTS FOR 4 SERVINGS

- 600 gr (3 cups) of ground turkey breast
- 100 gr (1 cup) of salami
- 60 gr (1/4 cup) of grated cheddar cheese
- 2 eggs
- 200 gr (7 oz) of boiled peas
- 2 spring onions
- 1 carrot
- 100 ml (half a glass) of Cognac
- 1 sprig of chopped parsley

- Breadcrumbs to taste
- Salt and pepper to taste
- Olive oil to taste

DIRECTIONS

1. Start by finely chopping the salami with a knife.
2. Remove the green part of the spring onions, wash the white part, and cut it into thin slices.
3. Put the spring onions, salami, turkey meat and 100 grams (1 cup) of peas in a bowl.
4. Stir with a fork and as soon as they are well blended, add the eggs, cheddar cheese, 3 tbsp of breadcrumbs, chopped parsley, salt and pepper.
5. Knead well and as soon as you have obtained a homogeneous mixture, form the meatloaf with your hands and then pass it on to the breadcrumbs.
6. Peel and wash the carrot and then cut it into cubes.
7. Take a disposable pan suitable for your fryer and brush it with a little oil.
8. Put the carrot, the remaining peas, and the chopped parsley at the bottom of the pan.
9. Season them with pepper and salt, and mix to flavor them well.
10. Now place the meatloaf on top and sprinkle everything with Cognac.
11. Cook the meatloaf at 200 °C (392°F) for 10 minutes. Turn it over and continue cooking for another 10/15 minutes, sprinkling it with the cooking juices and adding a little water if necessary.
12. Once ready, remove the meatloaf from the fryer and let it rest for 5 minutes.
13. Cut it into slices, put it on plates and sprinkle it with the vegetables and cooking juices.
14. You can serve.

44. **Thyme onion and bay roasted turkey**

PREPARATION TIME: 10 minutes
COOKING TIME: 20 minutes
CALORIES: 370
NUTRITIONAL VALUES: CARBS: 3 GR; PROTEINS: 38 GR; FATS: 2GR

INGREDIENTS FOR 4 SERVINGS
- 800 gr (28.2 oz) of turkey breast
- 8 bay leaves
- 4 sprigs of thyme
- 1 little onion
- 1 glass (200 ml) of white wine
- 400 ml (2 cups) of chicken broth
- Olive oil to taste
- Salt and pepper to taste

DIRECTIONS

1. Peel and wash the onion and cut it into slices.
2. Wash thyme and bay.
3. Wash and dry the turkey and remove any bones and excess fat.
4. Roll the turkey in kitchen twine.
5. Brush a pan with olive oil and put the turkey inside.
6. Add the onion, bay, and thyme.
7. Season with oil, salt and pepper, and sprinkle with the wine.
8. Place the pan in the air fryer and cook at 200 ° C (392°F) for 10 minutes.
9. After 10 minutes, turn the turkey and add the broth.
10. Cook for another 10 minutes.
11. Once cooked, remove the turkey from the air fryer and let it rest for a couple of minutes.
12. Place the turkey on the table and remove the kitchen string.
13. Cut the turkey breast into slices and place them on serving plates.
14. Sprinkle with the cooking juices and serve.

45. <u>Turkey chunks and potatoes</u>

PREPARATION TIME: 5 minutes
COOKING TIME: 20 minutes
CALORIES: 460

NUTRITIONAL VALUES: CARBS: 32 GR; PROTEIN: 30 GR; FATS: 12 GR

INGREDIENTS FOR 4 SERVINGS
- 600 gr (21.1 oz) of turkey breast
- 450 gr of potatoes (2 cups)
- 1 ½ tbsp of olive oil
- 2 tbsp of breadcrumbs
- 1 tsp of roast spices
- Salt to taste

DIRECTIONS

1. First, clean and cut the turkey breast into chunks.
2. Put the turkey meat in a bowl.
3. Peel the potatoes, wash and cut them into not too thick wedges. Season with a tablespoon and a half of olive oil and salt.
4. Add the breadcrumbs to the potatoes.
5. Add the potatoes to the turkey chunks and add spices as well. Using a wooden spoon, mix all the ingredients well.
6. Place them in the fryer basket (or in a suitable baking pan).
7. Turn on the fryer and program it for 15 minutes at 200 °C (392°F).
8. Halfway through cooking, remove the basket, turn the turkey meat and potatoes, and restart.
9. After the time has elapsed, the meat and the potatoes should be cooked. However, if not, cook for another 5 minutes.
10. Serve the turkey and potatoes hot.

Pork, beef, and lamb

Pork recipes

46. Ham and zucchini stuffed pork loin

PREPARATION TIME: 10 minutes
COOKING TIME: 20/22 minutes
CALORIES: 480
NUTRITIONAL VALUES: CARBS: 7 GR; PROTEINS: 40 GR; FATS: 26 GR

INGREDIENTS FOR 4 SERVINGS

- 1 pork loin of 800 grams (28.9 oz)
- 100 gr (3.5 oz) of cream cheese
- 1 big size zucchini
- 120 gr (1 cup) of cooked ham
- ½ shallot
- 1 tsp of marjoram leaves
- 100 ml (3.5 oz) of white wine
- 1 tbsp of cognac

- Olive oil to taste
- Salt and pepper to taste

DIRECTIONS

1. Let's start with the preparation of the pork loin. Remove any fat, make a central incision and divide the pork loin into two halves.
2. Make a lateral incision in both pork halves to obtain a kind of pocket.
3. Wash the pork loins, dry them with a paper towel and then sprinkle them with a little salt and pepper.
4. Now move on to the zucchini. Remove the ends, wash them under running water, and cut them into small cubes.
5. Peel the half shallot, wash it under running water, dry it and cut it into thin slices.
6. Put a tablespoon of olive oil in a suitable air fryer pan. Add the shallot and then the zucchini. Season with salt, add the marjoram and then let the zucchini cook in the air fryer for 6 minutes at 180°C (338°F).
7. Meanwhile, cut the cooked ham into small pieces.
8. Remove the zucchini from the air fryer. Let them cool and then add the cooked ham and the cream cheese. Mix well all the ingredients.
9. Take another baking dish and brush it with a drizzle of oil.

10. Take the pork fillets and fill with the zucchini filling. Close them with a toothpick.
11. Place the meat in the pan and sprinkle some oil on top of the pork.
12. Place the dish in the fryer basket. Set the temperature to 190 °C (375°F) for 8/10 minutes.
13. After the time has passed, take the basket out, turn the pork, sprinkle a little olive oil, and pour in the wine and cognac.
14. Cook for another 4 minutes. Always check the cooking, and if it still does not seem cooked, continue for another 2-3 minutes.
15. Serve the filled pork loin still hot.

47. **Peas and cheddar pork meatballs**

PREPARATION TIME: 15 minutes
COOKING TIME: 10 minutes
CALORIES: 400
NUTRITIONAL VALUES: CARBS: 16 GR; PROTEIN: 22 GR; FATS: 20 GR

INGREDIENTS FOR 4 SERVINGS
- 300 gr (10.5 oz) of minced pork
- 100 gr (3.5 oz) of already boiled peas
- 2 eggs
- 60 gr (1/4 cup) of grated cheddar cheese
- Milk to taste

- Breadcrumbs to taste
- Olive oil to taste
- Salt and pepper to taste

DIRECTIONS

1. Put the minced pork, an egg, cheddar cheese, salt and pepper into a bowl.
2. Mix the ingredients with a fork.
3. Now add the boiled peas and a bit of breadcrumbs. Mix first with a fork and then knead everything with your hands.
4. If the dough is soft, add a few more breadcrumbs. Instead, if it is too dry, add a few tablespoons of milk.
5. Moisten your hands with water and start forming the meatballs.
6. They must be about the size of a walnut.
7. Beat the other egg and put some breadcrumbs on a plate. First, put the meatballs in the egg and then roll them in breadcrumbs.
8. Place the pork meatballs well apart in the basket of the air fryer.
9. Sprinkle each meatball with olive oil, and set the fryer at 200° (392°F) for 5 minutes.
10. After 5 minutes, turn the meatballs, sprinkle a bit of oil, and cook for another 2-3 minutes.
11. If they still don't seem cooked, continue cooking for another 2 minutes until they are golden and crunchy.

12. Serve still hot with a favorite sauce.

48. <u>Pork loin with mozzarella</u>

PREPARATION TIME: 10 minutes
COOKING TIME: 15 minutes
CALORIES: 430
NUTRITIONAL VALUES: CARBS: 7 GR; PROTEINS: 35 GR; FATS: 22 GR

INGREDIENTS FOR 4 SERVINGS

- 4 slices of pork loin (600 grams or 3 cups)
- 10 gr (1 tbsp) of butter
- 4 ripe tomatoes
- 2 mozzarellas
- 1 tsp of Dried oregano
- Flour to taste
- Olive oil to taste
- Salt and pepper to taste

DIRECTIONS

1. Start with the pork meat. Wash it quickly under running water, dry it with a paper towel, and set it aside.
2. Take a baking dish and lightly butter it.
3. Now flour the slices of pork loin and then place them in a suitable air fryer pan.
4. Wash and dry the tomatoes. Cut them into slices.

5. Cut the mozzarella into slices that are not too thick.
6. Mix 2 tablespoons of olive oil, salt, pepper, and oregano in a bowl.
7. Spread the tomato slices on each slice of the pork loin. Add a pinch of salt and pepper to the tomatoes and then cover with the mozzarella slices.
8. Sprinkle everything with oregano oil and place the pan in the fryer basket.
9. Cook at 200 °C (392°F) for 12/13 minutes.
10. Check the cooking, and if it still doesn't seem cooked, continue for another 2 minutes.
11. Serve piping hot and racy.

49. **Smoked cheese and bacon pork meatloaf**

PREPARATION TIME: 10 minutes
COOKING TIME: 20/25 minutes
CALORIES: 520
NUTRITIONAL VALUES: CARBS: 3 GR; PROTEINS: 31 GR; FATS: 40 GR

INGREDIENTS FOR 4 SERVINGS
- 400 gr (2 cups) of ground pork meat
- 200 gr (1 cup) of smoked cheese
- 60 ml (1/4 cup) of half and half
- 100 grams (3.5 oz) of smoked bacon
- 1 tsp of chopped sage
- ½ tsp of nutmeg
- Olive oil to taste
- Salt and pepper to taste

DIRECTIONS
1. Start with preparing the meat. Put the minced pork meat in a bowl, half and half, chopped bacon, diced smoked cheese, a pinch of nutmeg, chopped sage, salt and pepper.
2. Moisten your hands and form the meatloaf.
3. Take a large aluminum foil to hold the meatloaf and grease it with oil.
4. Arrange the pork meatloaf inside the aluminum foil and then close everything.
5. Place the packet inside the fryer basket and set it at 200 °C (392°F) for 20 minutes.
6. When the time has elapsed, check the cooking. If it still does not seem cooked enough, continue to cook for another 5 minutes with the aluminum foil open.
7. Remove the meatloaf from the fryer, let it cool, and cut it into slices.

50. **Spicy breaded pork chops**

PREPARATION TIME: 10 minutes
COOKING TIME: 15/20 minutes
CALORIES: 390

NUTRITIONAL VALUES: CARBS: 18 GR; PROTEINS: 19 GR; FATS: 22 GR

INGREDIENTS FOR 4 SERVINGS

- 4 boneless pork chops
- 120 gr (1 cup) of breadcrumbs
- 3 eggs
- 1 tsp of garlic powder
- 110 gr (1 cup) of flour
- 1 tsp of onions powder
- 1 tsp of powdered ginger
- 1 tsp of Tabasco sauce
- salt and white pepper to taste

DIRECTIONS

1. First, clean the pork chops and place them in a zip-lock bag or cover them with cling film.
2. Pound the meat with a rolling pin until it is thin.
3. Add the breadcrumbs and all spices (onion, garlic, and ginger) to a bowl, then mix everything well.
4. Beat the eggs in a dish together with Tabasco sauce.
5. Put the chops in the flour, then in the beaten eggs and finally, roll them in the breadcrumb mix.
6. Preheat the air fryer to 190 ° C (375°F).
7. Graze the pork with olive oil and place it in the preheated fryer.
8. Cook the pork chops at 180 ° C (356°F). for 15 minutes, checking the cooking.
9. Remove from fryer when cooked and let stand for 5 minutes.
10. Cut into pieces and serve.

51. **Thyme and brandy pork loin**

PREPARATION TIME: 5 minutes
COOKING TIME: 40 minutes
CALORIES: 390
NUTRITIONAL VALUES: CARBS: 1 GR; PROTEINS: 28 GR; FATS: 16 GR

INGREDIENTS FOR 4 SERVINGS

- 700 gr (24.6 oz) of whole lean pork loin
- 2 tsp of olive oil
- 2 tsp of chopped thyme
- ½ glass (100 ml) of Brandy
- Salt and black pepper to taste

DIRECTIONS

1. First, clean and season the pork meat with salt, pepper, and oil. Put the meat in a non-stick pan greased with oil and seal all sides.
2. Deglaze with the glass of brandy.
3. Transfer the roast pork to a disposable pan the diameter of the fryer basket and pour the sauce that has formed into the pan.
4. Put the 2 tsp of washed and chopped thyme on the meat.

5. Set the fryer's temperature to 200° C (392°F) and cook for about 35/40 minutes, checking and turning the meat during cooking.

6. When the cooking time is reached, remove the roast pork from the pan. Let it cool, then cut it into thin slices.

7. Season the slices of meat with the sauce remaining in the pan and serve.

52. <u>Zucchini and peas pork loin</u>

PREPARATION TIME: 10 minutes
COOKING TIME: 10/15 minutes
CALORIES: 540
NUTRITIONAL VALUES: CARBS: 21 GR; PROTEINS: 41 GR; FATS: 22 GR

INGREDIENTS FOR 4 SERVINGS
- 1 kg (2.2 lbs) of sliced Pork fillet
- 2 tbsp of White wine
- 400 gr (2 cups) of Peas
- 400 gr (2 cups) of zucchini
- Sage to taste
- Rosemary to taste
- Olive oil to taste
- Salt to taste.

DIRECTIONS
1. First, wash and Salt the pork slices on both sides.

2. Meanwhile, prepare the vegetables: boil the peas and clean and cut the zucchini into slices.

3. Now put the roast with vegetables in a disposable mold measuring your air fryer (which you have previously preheated) and pour over the white wine.

4. Sprinkle with the washed and chopped rosemary and sage.

5. Let cook all ingredients at 200 °C (392°F) for 10/15 minutes, always checking the cooking and shaking the basket from time to time.

6. Serve the roast with all vegetables hot.

Beef

53. <u>Bacon and peppers beef meatloaf</u>

PREPARATION TIME: 10 minutes
COOKING TIME: 35 minutes
CALORIES: 580
NUTRITIONAL VALUES: CARBS: 14 GR; PROTEINS: 32 GR; FATS: 30 GR

INGREDIENTS FOR 4 SERVINGS
- 700 gr (24.6 oz) of lean ground beef
- 100 gr (1/2 cup) of breadcrumbs
- 100 ml (1/2 cup) of milk
- 1 egg
- 1 red bell pepper

- 120 gr (1/2 cup) of shredded provolone cheese
- 100 gr (3.5 oz) of bacon
- 1 tsp of onion powder
- Olive oil to taste
- Salt and pepper to taste

DIRECTIONS

1. First, wash the pepper and put it in the air fryer basket at 180 °C (338°F) for 10 minutes.
2. Remove the pepper from the deep fryer and let it cool.
3. Meanwhile, put the beef in a bowl.
4. Add the milk, egg, breadcrumbs, onion powder, salt and pepper, and mix well.
5. Put the slices of bacon on top of a large sheet of parchment paper, and then put the dough in the center.
6. Roll it out with your hands until you get a rectangle.
7. At this point, take the pepper, peel it, remove the stalk, seeds and white filaments, and cut it into slices.
8. Put the slices of pepper on the meat and add the shredded provolone cheese.
9. Roll the meat over the filling with the parchment paper.
10. Tie the meatloaf with kitchen string and brush it with olive oil.
11. Put the meatloaf in the basket and cook at 190°C (375°F) for 10 minutes.

12. After 10 minutes, turn it, brush it with a little more oil and cook for another 10 minutes.
13. Once the meatloaf is cooked, remove it from the fryer and let it thicken for 5 minutes on a cutting board.
14. Cut the meatloaf into slices, put it on serving plates and serve.

54. <u>Marjoram and shallot beef chops</u>

PREPARATION TIME: 5 minutes
COOKING TIME: 8/10 minutes
CALORIES: 210
NUTRITIONAL VALUES: CARBS: 1 GR; PROTEINS: 24 GR; FATS: 9 GR

INGREDIENTS FOR 4 SERVINGS

- 4 beef chops
- 1 little shallot
- 1 tablespoon of olive oil
- 2 teaspoons of chopped marjoram
- Salt and pepper to taste

DIRECTIONS

1. Turn on the air fryer and let it heat up by setting the temperature to 180 ° C (338°f).
2. Put the shallot strips in cold water for at least 5 minutes.

3. Put the shallot strips, salt, pepper, washed and chopped marjoram and olive oil directly on the meat.
4. Place the meat in the basket of the air fryer.
5. Set the cooking timer to 10 minutes (always keep an eye on cooking the meat and the shallot strips).
6. Serve the dish still warm.

55. Orange and rosemary beef roast

PREPARATION TIME: 50 minutes
COOKING TIME: 30 minutes
CALORIES: 220
NUTRITIONAL VALUES: CARBS: 6 GR; PROTEINS: 23 GR; FATS: 10 GR

INGREDIENTS FOR 4 SERVINGS
- 600 grams (3 cups) of beef fillet
- 1 large orange
- 1 sprig of rosemary
- ½ teaspoon of corn starch
- 1 tbsp of extra virgin olive oil
- 100 ml (1/2 glass) of white wine
- Salt and pepper to taste

DIRECTIONS
1. First, wash and dry the orange well.
2. Finely grate the orange peel and squeeze the juice.

3. Mix the juice and orange peel with rosemary, white wine, salt and pepper in a baking dish.
4. Then mix well with the rosemary sprigs and add the beef meat.
5. Leave it to marinate for 45-50 minutes, turning it often in the liquid.
6. Transfer the beef with the marinade and insert it into the air fryer at 200° C (392°F) for 25/30 minutes.
7. Turn the meat after 15 minutes, and occasionally sprinkle it with its sauce. If it gets dark or too dry, cover it.
8. When cooked, strain the sauce, and put it in a saucepan.
9. When it is warm, add a tablespoon of sifted cornstarch and mix well with a fork to avoid the formation of lumps.
10. Heat over medium heat and let it thicken. Then add a pinch salt and pepper.
11. Serve the sliced orange beef fillet with its sauce.

56. Pomegranate sauce beef fillet

PREPARATION TIME: 10 minutes
COOKING TIME: 20 minutes
CALORIES: 290
NUTRITIONAL VALUES: CARBS: 8 GR; PROTEINS: 26 GR; FATS: 7 GR

INGREDIENTS FOR 4 SERVINGS

- 700 gr (24.6 oz) of lean beef fillet
- 400 ml (2 cups) of pomegranate juice extract
- 1 garlic clove
- rosemary to taste
- bay leaf to taste
- 60 gr (1/4 cup) of butter
- 2 tbsp of corn starch
- 1 tsp of sugar

DIRECTIONS

1. Wash and dry the beef fillet with a kitchen towel.
2. Wash all the aromatic herbs and peel the garlic clove.
3. Soak the beef fillet in pomegranate juice with garlic, rosemary, bay leaf, and pepper.
4. Cover with plastic wrap. Place in the fridge for about 2 hours and turn it from time to time.
5. Now, prepare the sauce by filtering the marinating juice, add the sugar and corn starch. Let the sauce thicken on the fire.
6. Place the fillet in the preheated air fryer at 180 ºC (338ºF) for about 12/15 minutes.
7. When it is cooked, cut the beef fillet into slices. Season with the pomegranate sauce, and serve.

57. Sweet and sour veggies beef

PREPARATION TIME: 15 minutes
COOKING TIME: 15 minutes
CALORIES: 290
NUTRITIONAL VALUES: CARBS: 7 GR; PROTEINS: 25 GR; FATS: 13 GR

INGREDIENTS FOR 4 SERVINGS

- 600 gr (21.1 oz) of sliced beef fillet
- 2 Zucchini
- 2 Carrots
- 1/2 onion
- 2 garlic cloves
- 1 tbsp of Honey
- 1 tbsp of soy sauce
- 2 tbsp of Apple cider vinegar
- A pinch of smoked paprika
- Olive oil to taste
- Salt to taste
- Parsley to taste

DIRECTIONS

1. Mix the apple cider vinegar, honey, soy sauce, a drizzle of oil and paprika in a large bowl.
2. Add the garlic and onion cut into small pieces, then add the cleaned and washed beef fillet.
3. Mix well so that the meat is flavored.
4. Leave to marinate for about 30 minutes, covering the bowl with plastic wrap.

5. Meanwhile, peel the zucchini and carrots, and cut them into sticks or slices.
6. Preheat the air fryer, grease it with a little oil, and cook the vegetables for 5/6 minutes at 200°C (392°F).
7. Move them often, so they do not burn; they must remain tasty and consistent without falling apart.
8. When they are almost ready, drain the fillet and put it to cook in the same basket, wetting the bottom with a little of the liquid from the marinade. It will take about 5 minutes, depending on the thickness, to raise the temperature to 200°C (392°F) in grill mode and turn the beef meat on both sides
9. When cooked, add a handful of chopped parsley, and serve your sweet and sour beef dish.

58. <u>Swiss Cheese spicy beef meatballs</u>

PREPARATION TIME: 10 minutes
COOKING TIME: 10 minutes
CALORIES: 260
NUTRITIONAL VALUES: CARBS: 3 GR; PROTEINS: 22 GR; FATS: 15 GR

INGREDIENTS FOR 2 SERVINGS
- 500 gr (1.1 lbs) of ground beef
- 1 tsp of salt
- black pepper to taste
- 1 tsp of Worcestershire sauce
- 1 tsp of chopped jalapeno
- 1 tbsp of mustard
- 1 tbsp of grated onion
- 1 beaten egg
- 30 ml (2 tbsp) of olive oil
- 4 slices of Swiss cheese

DIRECTIONS
1. Mix the ground beef, pepper, salt, chopped jalapeno, Worcestershire sauce, grated onion, mustard, and egg together until well blended.
2. Form 8 beef patties and let them rest in the refrigerator for at least 40 minutes.
3. Preheat the air fryer to 180°C (338°F).
4. Rub the meatballs with olive oil and place them directly in the preheated fryer basket.
5. Set the time to about 8/10 minutes and let cook the beef meatballs.
6. Flip the meatballs after 5 minutes to ensure even cooking.
7. Add the slices of Swiss cheese to each meatball when there is 1/2 minute of cooking so that they melt.
8. Serve your cheesy meatballs still hot.

Lamb

59. Artichoke and eggplant roast lamb

PREPARATION TIME: 15 minutes
COOKING TIME: 45 minutes
CALORIES: 620
NUTRITIONAL VALUES: CARBOHYDRATES: 20 GR; PROTEIN: 34 GR; FATS: 31 GR

INGREDIENTS FOR 4 SERVINGS

- A 800 grams (1,8 lbs) lean leg of boneless lamb
- 4 artichokes
- 400 grams (2 cups) of eggplant
- 30 grams (2 tbsp) of pine nuts
- 2 sprigs of rosemary
- ½ glass of water
- 4 coriander leaves
- Olive oil to taste
- Salt and Pepper To Taste

DIRECTIONS

1. First, take the artichokes, remove the stem and the harder outer leaves, cut them into 4 parts, and remove the inner beard.
2. Peel the eggplants, wash them and then cut them into small cubes.
3. Wash and dry the coriander leaves and chop them.
4. Put a tablespoon of olive oil in a pan and as soon as it is hot, add the eggplant cubes, artichokes, coriander, pine nuts and half a glass of water.
5. Stir, add a pinch of salt and pepper, and cook for 15 minutes.
6. Wash and dry the rosemary.
7. Wash and dry the leg of the lamb and then cut it in half.
8. Add salt, pepper and rosemary to the lamb, and then add the filling.
9. Roll the leg up and secure it with kitchen twine.
10. Brush with olive oil and place it directly in the fryer basket.
11. Cook at 190 ° (375°F) for 15 minutes and then turn the meat.
12. Keep on cooking for another 10 minutes.
13. Once the lamb is cooked, remove it from the fryer and let it rest for 5 minutes.
14. Cut the lamb into slices, put them on serving plates and serve.

60. Broad beans and sweet potatoes lamb

PREPARATION TIME: 10 minutes
COOKING TIME: 20 minutes
CALORIES: 740
NUTRITIONAL VALUES: CARBS: 35 GR; PROTEINS: 40 GR; FATS: 32 GR

INGREDIENTS FOR 4 SERVINGS

- 700 grams (24.6 oz) of lamb pieces

- 8 sweet potatoes
- 200 grams (1 cup) of broad beans
- 200 ml (1 cup) of white wine
- Salt and Pepper To Taste.
- Olive oil to taste

DIRECTIONS

1. Peel the sweet potatoes and wash them under running water. Cut them into cubes.
2. Wash the broad beans and then let them drain.
3. Put the potatoes and broad beans in a bowl and season with oil, salt and pepper.
4. Brush a pan suitable for your fryer with olive oil and then put the sweet potatoes and broad beans inside the pan.
5. Wash and dry the lamb. Sprinkle the meat with pepper and salt and then place it in the pan.
6. Sprinkle everything with the wine and then put the pan in the fryer.
7. Cook at 200 ° (392°F) for 10 minutes, stir, then turn the meat and continue cooking for another 10 minutes. If you're not satisfied, check the cooking and keep cooking for another 5 minutes.
8. Once the meat is cooked, remove it from the fryer and let the meat rest for 5 minutes.
9. Place the lamb on the plates, garnish with the sweet potatoes and broad beans and serve.

61. Crackers breadcrumbs crispy lamb chops

PREPARATION TIME: 10 minutes
COOKING TIME: 16/18 minutes
CALORIES: 690
NUTRITIONAL VALUES: CARBS 23 GR; PROTEINS: 38 GR; FATS: 29 GR

INGREDIENTS FOR 4 SERVINGS

- 8 lamb chops
- 200 grams (7 oz) of saltine crackers
- 2 eggs
- 80 ml (1/3 cup) of coconut milk
- Olive oil to taste
- Salt and Pepper To Taste

DIRECTIONS

1. Start by washing and drying the lamb chops. Also, remove excess fat and thin them with a meat mallet.
2. Shell the eggs in a bowl. Add the coconut milk, salt and pepper and beat them with a fork.
3. Put the cutlets inside and let them soften for 30 minutes.
4. In the meantime, take the crackers, put them in the glass of the mixer,

and chop them until you get a fairly fine mixture.

5. Now put the chopped crackers on a plate.
6. After 30 minutes, pass the lamb chops over the crackers.
7. Place the ribs in the fryer basket and sprinkle olive oil on the surface.
8. Cook the ribs for 10 minutes at 200 °C (392°F), then turn them, sprinkle them with a bit of oil and continue cooking for another 6/8 minutes.
9. As soon as the chops are ready, remove them from the deep fryer and let them rest for 5 minutes.
10. Put them on the plates. Serve and enjoy.

62. <u>Creamy jalapeno lamb chops</u>

PREPARATION TIME: 15 minutes
COOKING TIME: 25/30 minutes
CALORIES: 490
NUTRITIONAL VALUES: CARBS: 10 GR; PROTEINS: 35 GR; FATS: 30 GR

INGREDIENTS FOR 4 SERVINGS
- 4 lamb chops of 150 grams for each (5.3 oz about)
- 2 tbsp of apple cider vinegar
- ½ shallot
- 1 lime
- 100 ml (1/2 cup) of half and half
- 4 tsp of brown sugar
- 1 chopped jalapeno
- Salt and Pepper To Taste
- Olive oil to taste

DIRECTIONS
1. First, peel and wash and chop the shallot.
2. Remove the excess fat from the chops, then wash and dry them.
3. Rub the surface of the chops with the shallot and then brush them with olive oil. Add a pinch of salt and pepper.
4. Put the chops directly into the basket of the air fryer. Cook at 190°C (375°F) for 16 minutes and turn the chops after 8 minutes.
5. Meanwhile, prepare the accompanying sauce.
6. Put the sugar, vinegar and filtered lime juice in a pan.
7. Caramelize over low heat until the sugar turns a dark amber color and then add the half and half.
8. Let the sauce thicken for about 10 minutes.
9. As soon as it has thickened, season with salt and pepper, add the jalapeno and mix well.
10. Once cooked, remove the chops from the fryer and let them rest for 5 minutes.

11. After 5 minutes, place them on serving plates, sprinkle them with the creamy jalapeno sauce and serve.

63. <u>Mint and raspberry sauce lamb</u>

PREPARATION TIME: 15 minutes
COOKING TIME: 15 minutes
CALORIES: 410
NUTRITIONAL VALUES: CARBS: 10 GR; PROTEINS: 30 GR; FATS: 22 GR

INGREDIENTS FOR 4 SERVINGS

- 600 grams (3 cups about) of lamb chops
- 200 grams (1 cup) of raspberries
- 1 garlic clove
- 210 ml (1 cup) of Rum
- 60 ml (1/4 cup) of apple cider vinegar
- 2 tsp of chopped mint
- Olive oil to taste
- Salt and Pepper

DIRECTIONS

1. First, wash the raspberries, dry them, and put them in the blender glass.
2. Blend at high speed until the raspberries are completely dissolved.
3. Pass the raspberry juice into a colander and collect it in a bowl.
4. Wash the lamb chops and dry them.
5. Peel and wash the garlic and then chop it.
6. Put the rum, mint leaves, apple cider vinegar, and minced garlic in the bowl and mix well.
7. Add a pinch of pepper and salt, and then add the chops.
8. Cover the bowl with cling film. Leave to marinate for an hour.
9. After the hour, brush an air fryer suitable baking pan with oil, and put the chops and all the bowl contents inside.
10. Place the pan inside the fryer and cook at 200°C (392°F) for 8 minutes.
11. After 7 minutes, turn the chops and continue cooking for another 7 minutes.
12. Once cooked, remove the pan from the air fryer.
13. Let it rest for 5 minutes, then put the chops on serving plates.
14. Sprinkle with the cooking juices and then sprinkle the surface with a bit of pepper.
15. You can serve.

64. <u>Sherry and bay lamb chops</u>

PREPARATION TIME: 10 minutes
COOKING TIME: 20 minutes

CALORIES: 430
NUTRITIONAL VALUES: CARBS: 6 GR; PROTEINS: 31 GR; FATS: 25 GR

INGREDIENTS FOR 4 SERVINGS

- 4 Lamb chops (700 grams of 1,5 oz)
- A glass of Sherry
- 2 tbsp of barbecue sauce
- 1 tsp of chopped bay leaves
- 2 tbsp of olive oil
- Salt to taste.

DIRECTIONS

1. First, wash the lamb ribs under running water, then dry them with a paper towel.
2. Put the cutlets, sherry, oil, barbecue sauce, bay leaves and salt in a bowl.
3. Turn the chops, so they absorb salt and liquid.
4. Preheat the deep fryer for a few minutes at 200 ° C (392°F).
5. Place them in the fryer and start at 200 ° for 20 minutes, turning them 3-4 times during cooking.
6. Serve the sherry lamb still hot.

65. <u>Walnuts and almond crust Rack of lamb</u>

PREPARATION TIME: 10 minutes
COOKING TIME: 25 minutes

CALORIES: 460
NUTRITIONAL VALUES: CARBS: 12 GR; PROTEINS: 32 GR; FATS: 26 GR

INGREDIENTS FOR 4 SERVINGS

- 600 grams (1,3 lbs) of rack of lamb
- 1 tbsp of olive oil
- 30 grams (2 tbsp) of almonds
- 30 grams (2 tbsp) of walnuts
- 1 big egg
- 1 small orange
- 1 tsp of chopped mint
- 1 tsp of chopped basil
- 100 grams (1/2 cup) of breadcrumbs
- Salt and black pepper to taste

DIRECTIONS

1. First, wash the lamb ribs under running water, then dry them with a paper towel.
2. Toast the almonds and shelled walnuts in an oil-free pan for 2-3 minutes until they turn dark brown, then let them cool.
3. When they have cooled, chop them very finely.
4. Wash the orange and grate two teaspoons of zest.
5. Blend the almonds, walnuts, orange zest, mint, basil, breadcrumbs, and egg, then add a pinch of salt and pepper.
6. Preheat the air fryer to 200 ° C (392°F).

7. Season the rack of lamb with salt and pepper to taste.
8. Place the rack of lamb on a baking sheet (suitable for the air fryer) with the bones facing up, then sprinkle it on both sides with the almond, walnuts, and herb mixture.
9. Cook for about 20 minutes and check the cooking.
10. Let the meat rest for 10 minutes after taking it out of the air fryer and serve.

Fish and seafood

66. <u>Cod au gratin</u>

PREPARATION TIME: 10 minutes
COOKING TIME: 12 minutes
CALORIES: 360

NUTRITIONAL VALUES: CARBS: 28 GR; PROTEINS: 32 GR; FATS: 12 GR

INGREDIENTS FOR 4 SERVINGS
- 800 gr (1,8 lbs) of cod fillet
- 100 gr (3.5 oz of breadcrumbs)
- 1 clove of minced garlic
- 2 anchovy fillets
- Chopped parsley to taste
- Salt and pepper to taste
- Olive oil to taste

DIRECTIONS
1. Wash the cod fillet, remove the bones and skin, and then cut it into 8 smaller fillets.
2. Mix the breadcrumbs, salt, pepper, chopped anchovies, parsley, incet garlic, and olive oil in a bowl.

3. Brush the cod fillets with olive oil and place them in the air fryer basket.
4. Sprinkle the surface of the cod with the breadcrumbs and close the air fryer.
5. Cook at 180 ° C (356 ° F) for 12 minutes.
6. Once cooked, take the cod fillets from the air fryer, place them on plates, and serve.

67. Cod with potatoes and olives

PREPARATION TIME: 15 minutes
COOKING TIME: 25 minutes
CALORIES: 420
NUTRITIONAL VALUES: CARBS: 15 GR; PROTEINS: 38 GR; FATS: 16 GR

INGREDIENTS FOR 4 SERVINGS
- 4 cod fillets of 200 gr (7 oz) each
- 700 gr (24.6 oz) of potatoes
- 80 gr (2.8 oz) of black olives
- 50 gr (1.7 oz) of chopped and toasted hazelnuts
- Chopped parsley to taste
- ½ red onion
- 1 sprig of rosemary
- Salt and pepper to taste
- Olive oil to taste

DIRECTIONS
1. Wash and dry the cod and remove skin and bones.
2. Peel the potatoes, wash them, and cut them into thin slices.
3. Peel the onion and cut it into slices.
4. Brush a baking pan with oil and put the potato slices on the bottom and the onion on top.
5. Season with oil, salt, and pepper, add the rosemary and put the baking pan in the air fryer.
6. Cook at 180 ° C (356 ° F) for 15 minutes.
7. After 15 minutes, add the olives, cod fillets, salt and pepper, and brush with olive oil. Continue cooking for another 10 minutes.
8. Once cooked, remove the cod from the air fryer.
9. Put the cod fillets on the plates and add the potatoes and olives.
10. Sprinkle with the chopped hazelnuts and chopped parsley, and serve.

68. Haddock fillets with potatoes

PREPARATION TIME: 20 minutes
COOKING TIME: 20 minutes
CALORIES: 552
NUTRITIONAL VALUES: CARBS: 21 GR; PROTEINS: 33 GR; FATS: 12 GR

INGREDIENTS FOR 4 SERVINGS

- 4 haddock fillets of 200 gr (7 oz) each
- 600 g (21 oz) of potatoes
- 1 lemon
- Chopped parsley to taste
- Salt and pepper to taste
- Olive oil to taste

DIRECTIONS

1. Wash and dry the haddock fillets.
2. Peel the potatoes, wash, and cut them into cubes.
3. Place the potatoes in the air fryer's basket and place the haddock fillets on top.
4. Season with oil, salt, pepper, and lemon juice and close the air fryer.
5. Cook at 200 ° C (392 ° F) for 20 minutes, turning the fish after 10 minutes.
6. After cooking, take the haddock and potatoes and place them on serving plates.
7. Sprinkle with chopped parsley and serve.

69. Haddock fillets with pumpkin

PREPARATION TIME: 20 minutes
COOKING TIME: 20 minutes
CALORIES: 490
NUTRITIONAL VALUES: CARBS: 17 GR; PROTEINS: 42 GR; FATS: 16 GR

INGREDIENTS FOR 4 SERVINGS

- 4 haddock fillets of 200 gr (7 oz) each
- 600 gr of pumpkin pulp
- The grated zest of half a lemon
- 2 cloves of minced garlic
- 8 chopped basil leaves
- Salt and pepper to taste
- Olive oil to taste

DIRECTIONS

1. Wash and dry the haddock fillets.
2. Wash the pumpkin pulp and cut it into cubes.
3. Brush a baking pan with oil and put the pumpkin pulp on the bottom.
4. Add the haddock fillets and season with oil, salt, and pepper.
5. Sprinkle with basil, garlic and lemon zest and place the baking pan inside the air fryer.
6. Cook at 180 ° C (356 ° F) for 20 minutes, turning the fish after 10 minutes.
7. When the fish is cooked, take it out of the air fryer and place it on serving plates.
8. Add the pumpkin and serve.

70. Haddock in an herb crust

PREPARATION TIME: 10 minutes
COOKING TIME: 15 minutes

CALORIES: 301
NUTRITIONAL VALUES: CARBS: 21
GR; PROTEINS: 38 GR; FATS: 15 GR

INGREDIENTS FOR 4 SERVINGS

- 4 haddock fillets of 200 gr (7 oz) each
- 1 lemon
- 2 sprigs of thyme
- 2 sprigs of marjoram
- 100 g (7 oz) of breadcrumbs
- 1 sprig of chopped parsley
- 1 clove of minced garlic
- Olive oil to taste
- Salt and pepper to taste

DIRECTIONS

1. Wash the thyme and marjoram, chop them, and put them in a bowl.
2. Add the garlic, parsley, lemon juice, salt, pepper and 4 tablespoons of olive oil and mix well.
3. Wash and dry the haddock fillets, brush them with olive oil, and put them in the air fryer.
4. Sprinkle the fish with the herb breadcrumbs and close the air fryer.
5. Cook at 180 ° C (356 ° F) for 15 minutes.
6. After cooking, take the haddock from the air fryer, put it on plates, and serve.

71. **Halibut with capers**

PREPARATION TIME: 10 minutes
COOKING TIME: 12 minutes
CALORIES: 353
NUTRITIONAL VALUES: CARBS: 3
GR; PROTEINS: 42 GR; FATS: 12 GR

INGREDIENTS FOR 4 SERVINGS

- 8 halibut fillets of 100 gr (3.5 oz) each
- 1 clove of minced garlic
- ½ glass of white wine
- 3 tbsp of capers
- Salt and pepper to taste
- Olive oil to taste

DIRECTIONS

1. Wash and dry the halibut fillets.
2. Brush the halibut with olive oil and white wine. Add a pinch of salt and pepper.
3. Place the fish in the air fryer, and cook at 180 ° C (356 ° F) for 12 minutes, turning the fish after 6 minutes.
4. Meanwhile, prepare the caper sauce.
5. Rinse and squeeze the capers and put them in the mixer.
6. Add salt, pepper, garlic and 2 tablespoons of olive oil.
7. Operate the mixer and chop until you get a dense and homogeneous sauce.

8. Once cooked, take the halibut fillets from the air fryer, and place them on serving plates.
9. Sprinkle the halibut with the caper sauce and serve.

72. <u>Salmon fillets in maple syrup</u>

PREPARATION TIME: 10 minutes
COOKING TIME: 15 minutes
CALORIES: 365
NUTRITIONAL VALUES: CARBS: 14 GR; PROTEINS: 46 GR; FATS: 22 GR

INGREDIENTS FOR 4 SERVINGS

- 4 salmon fillets of 200 gr (7 oz)
- 80 ml (¼ cup) of maple syrup
- 1 clove of minced garlic
- 2 tbsp of soy sauce
- Olive oil to taste
- Salt and pepper to taste

DIRECTIONS

1. Wash the salmon fillets and remove all the bones.
2. Brush a baking pan with olive oil and put the salmon fillets inside.
3. Put the maple syrup in a bowl and add 3 tablespoons of olive oil, garlic, salt, pepper, and soy sauce. Mix well until you get a homogeneous emulsion.
4. Pour the emulsion over the salmon and put the baking pan in the air fryer.
5. Cook at 180 ° C (356 ° F) for 15 minutes, turning the salmon after 8 minutes.
6. Once cooked, remove the baking pan from the air fryer and let the salmon rest for a couple of minutes.
7. Now put the salmon on the plates, and sprinkle it with the cooking juices. Serve and enjoy!

73. <u>Salmon in green sauce</u>

PREPARATION TIME: 15 minutes
COOKING TIME: 10 minutes
CALORIES: 328
NUTRITIONAL VALUES: CARBS: 2 GR; PROTEINS: 34 GR; FATS: 18 GR

INGREDIENTS FOR 4 SERVINGS

- 800 gr (1,8 lbs) of salmon fillet
- 1 lemon
- 4 tbsp of chopped parsley
- Olive oil to taste
- Salt and pepper to taste

DIRECTIONS

1. Wash the salmon, remove the skin and bones, and cut the fillet into 8 slices of the same size.

2. Brush the salmon steaks with olive oil. Add a pinch of salt and pepper.
3. Place the salmon in the air fryer and cook at 180 ° C (356 ° F) for 10 minutes, turning the fish after 5 minutes.
4. Meanwhile, put the parsley, lemon juice, salt, pepper, and olive oil in the blender glass.
5. Operate the blender and blend until you get a dense and homogeneous sauce.
6. Once cooked, take the salmon steaks from the air fryer, and place them on the plates.
7. Sprinkle with the green sauce and serve.

74. <u>Salmon in tandoori sauce</u>

PREPARATION TIME: 15 minutes
COOKING TIME: 15 minutes
CALORIES: 413
NUTRITIONAL VALUES: CARBS: 5 GR; PROTEINS: 39 GR; FATS: 22 GR

INGREDIENTS FOR 4 SERVINGS
- 4 salmon fillets of 200 gr (7 oz) each
- 150 gr (5.2 oz) of Greek yogurt
- 100 gr (3.5 oz) of tandoori pasta
- ½ lemon
- ½ tsp of curry powder
- ½ tsp of ginger powder

- Salt to taste
- Olive oil to taste

DIRECTIONS
1. In a bowl, mix the tandoori paste, ginger, and curry.
2. Now add the Greek yogurt and the lemon juice, and mix.
3. Pour half of the mixture into a baking pan and add the salmon, washed, and boned.
4. Season the salmon with the salt and cover it with the rest of the sauce.
5. Place the baking pan in the air fryer and cook at 180 ° C (356 ° F) for 15 minutes, turning the salmon halfway through cooking.
6. Once cooked, remove the salmon from the air fryer, place it on plates, sprinkle it with the cooking juices, and serve.

75. <u>Salmon with asparagus and honey and mustard sauce</u>

PREPARATION TIME: 20 minutes
COOKING TIME: 15 minutes
CALORIES: 488
NUTRITIONAL VALUES: CARBS: 12 GR; PROTEINS: 38 GR; FATS: 32 GR
INGREDIENTS FOR 4 SERVINGS
- 4 salmon fillets of 150 gr (5.2 oz) each

- 400 gr (14 oz) of asparagus
- 1 lemon
- 3 tbsp of mustard
- 1 tsp of honey
- 250 ml (1 cup) of cooking cream
- ½ tsp of turmeric powder
- Salt and pepper to taste
- Olive oil to taste

DIRECTIONS

1. Wash the asparagus, remove the hardest part of the stem, and put them in a baking pan brushed with olive oil.
2. Wash the salmon fillets, remove the skin and bones, and place them on the asparagus.
3. Season everything with oil, salt, pepper, and lemon juice.
4. Place the baking pan in the air fryer and cook at 180 ° C (356 ° F) for 15 minutes, turning the fish after 8 minutes.
5. Meanwhile, make the honey mustard sauce.
6. Put the honey, cooking cream, mustard, some olive oil, salt, pepper, and turmeric in a bowl. Stir until you get a dense and homogeneous sauce.
7. Once the salmon is cooked, take the baking pan out of the air fryer.
8. Put the asparagus and salmon on the plates, sprinkle with the honey mustard sauce and serve.

76. <u>Sea bass with citrus and pomegranate</u>

PREPARATION TIME: 15 minutes
COOKING TIME: 12 minutes
CALORIES: 278
NUTRITIONAL VALUES: CARBS: 12 GR; PROTEINS: 32 GR; FATS: 8 GR

INGREDIENTS FOR 4 SERVINGS

- 4 sea bass fillets of 200 gr (7oz) each
- 1 orange
- 4 tbsp of pomegranate grains
- 1 clove of minced garlic
- 2 sprigs of marjoram
- 1 sprig of thyme
- Salt and pepper to taste
- Olive oil to taste

DIRECTIONS

1. Wash and dry the sea bass and remove all the bones.
2. Peel the orange and cut the pulp into pieces.
3. Wash and dry the marjoram and thyme and then chop them.
4. Brush a baking pan with olive oil and put the sea bass inside.
5. Add the orange, pomegranate seeds, oil, salt, pepper, thyme, marjoram, and garlic.
6. Place the baking pan in the air fryer and cook at 200 ° C (392 ° F) for 12

minutes, turning the fish halfway through cooking.

7. After cooking, take the sea bass from the air fryer and place it on serving plates.
8. Sprinkle with oranges and pomegranate grains, and serve.

77. **Sea bream with potatoes and pumpkin baked in foil**

PREPARATION TIME: 15 minutes
COOKING TIME: 30 minutes
CALORIES: 368
NUTRITIONAL VALUES: CARBS: 21 GR; PROTEINS: 48 GR; FATS: 7 GR

INGREDIENTS FOR 4 SERVINGS
- 4 sea bream fillets of 250 gr (8.8 oz) each
- 4 potatoes
- 200 gr (7 oz) of pumpkin pulp
- 1 lemon
- 1 clove of minced garlic
- Chopped parsley to taste
- Salt and pepper to taste
- Olive oil to taste

DIRECTIONS
1. Wash the sea bream fillets and remove all the bones.
2. Peel the potatoes, wash them, and cut them into thin slices.
3. Wash the pumpkin pulp and cut it into thin slices the same size as the potatoes.
4. Take 4 sheets of parchment paper and brush them with olive oil.
5. Put the potatoes and pumpkin on the bottom, and then add oil, salt, and pepper.
6. Put the seabream fillets on top and then add salt, pepper, and lemon juice.
7. Sprinkle with chopped parsley and garlic, and close the sheets of parchment paper.
8. Place the fish in the air fryer, and cook at 180 ° C (356 ° F) for 30 minutes.
9. After cooking, remove the fish from the air fryer.
10. Put the fish bags on the serving plates, open them carefully and serve.

78. **Tilapia with pistachios**

PREPARATION TIME: 10 minutes
COOKING TIME: 15 minutes
CALORIES: 399
NUTRITIONAL VALUES: CARBS: 18 GR; PROTEINS: 41 GR; FATS: 17 GR

INGREDIENTS FOR 4 SERVINGS

- 4 fillets of tilapia of 200 gr (7 oz) each
- 75 gr (2.6 oz) of flour
- 1 lemon
- 3 tbsp of chopped pistachios
- Salt and pepper to taste
- Olive oil to taste

DIRECTIONS

1. Wash the tilapia fillets and them.
2. Put the flour, salt and pepper on a plate and flour the tilapia fillets well on both sides.
3. Wash the lemon, cut it into slices and place it on the bottom of a baking pan brushed with olive oil.
4. Place the tilapia fillets on top, sprinkle with olive oil, and place the baking pan in the air fryer.
5. Cook at 180 ° C (356 ° F) for 8 minutes. Flip the fish and sprinkle with chopped pistachios. Continue cooking for another 7 minutes.
6. After cooking, take the baking pan from the air fryer, put the tilapia and lemon slices on the plates, and serve.

79. <u>Trout with potatoes and cherry tomatoes</u>

PREPARATION TIME: 15 minutes
COOKING TIME: 20 minutes

CALORIES: 379
NUTRITIONAL VALUES: CARBS: 24 GR; PROTEINS: 36 GR; FATS: 10 GR

INGREDIENTS FOR 4 SERVINGS

- 4 trout fillets of 250 gr (8.8 oz) each
- 600 gr (21 oz) of potatoes
- 1 red onion
- 300 gr (10.5 oz) of tomatoes
- 1 lemon
- Salt and pepper to taste
- Olive oil to taste

DIRECTIONS

1. Wash the trout fillets and remove the bones.
2. Peel the potatoes, wash them, and cut them into cubes.
3. Peel the onion and cut it into slices.
4. Wash the tomatoes and cut them into slices.
5. Brush a baking pan and put the potatoes, tomatoes, and onion on the bottom.
6. Add oil, salt and pepper, and then put the trout fillets on top.
7. Season the trout with oil, salt, pepper, and lemon juice, and put the baking pan in the air fryer.
8. Cook at 200 ° (392 ° F) for 20 minutes, turning the trout after 10 minutes.
9. When the trout is cooked, take it out of the air fryer and place it on the plates.
10. Add the potatoes, onion and tomatoes, and serve.

Vegetarian Mains

80. <u>Artichoke and smoked cheese omelette</u>

PREPARATION TIME: 15 minutes
COOKING TIME: 14/16 minutes
CALORIES: 320
NUTRITIONAL VALUES: CARBS: 8
GR PROTEINS: 34 GR FATS: 11 GR

INGREDIENTS FOR 4 SERVINGS

- 5 eggs
- 4 artichokes heart
- 1 lemon
- 80 gr (1/3 cup) of grated smoked cheese
- 1 tbsp of olive oil
- Salt and black pepper
- chopped parsley to taste

DIRECTIONS

1. First, remove the hard outer leaves and cut off the upper part of the more tender leaves.
2. In this way, you will get 4 artichoke hearts.
3. Put them in a pot with salted water and a piece of lemon and bring them to a boil.
4. Boil them for about 10 minutes.
5. In the end, drain them.
6. Meanwhile, beat the eggs in a bowl with a pinch of salt and pepper.
7. Now you can add the olive oil and a pinch of chopped parsley.
8. Also, add the boiled or raw artichokes cut into thin slices and mix.
9. Pour half the omelette dough into the pan and place the grated smoked cheese in the center.
10. Cover the filling with the rest of the dough.
11. Transfer it to the preheated air fryer at 200° C (392°F) and cook for about 14/16 minutes.
12. Always check the cooking status.
13. Once cooked, take the omelette out of the air fryer. Serve it in slices with chopped parsley on the surface.

81. Battered zucchini

PREPARATION TIME: 10 minutes
COOKING TIME: 8/10 minutes

CALORIES: 150
NUTRITIONAL VALUES: CARBS: 12 GR; PROTEIN: 6 GR; FATS: 9 GR

INGREDIENTS FOR 4 SERVINGS

- 2 medium size zucchinis, cut into strips
- 80 gr (1/3 cup) of all-purpose flour
- 1 tbsp of salt
- 80 gr (1/3 cup) of breadcrumbs
- 1 tsp of black pepper
- 2 eggs
- 15 ml (1 tbsp) of milk
- 2 tbsp of grated Parmesan cheese

DIRECTIONS

1. First, peel, wash and cut the zucchini into medium-thick strips.
2. Put the all-purpose flour, salt, and pepper in a dish, and mix well.
3. Beat the eggs and milk together on a separate plate.
4. Put the breadcrumbs and Parmesan in another dish, and mix well.
5. Cover the zucchini with flour, dip them in the egg, and roll them in breadcrumbs.
6. Preheat a few minutes at 180 ° C (338°F).
7. Place the evenly coated zucchini in the air fryer and spray with non-stick cooking spray.
8. Set the time to 8/10 minutes.
9. Shake the fryer basket halfway through cooking.

10. Serve the battered zucchini with mayonnaise, mustard, or a sauce of your choice.

82. Broccoli and cheddar flan

PREPARATION TIME: 15 minutes
COOKING TIME: 30 minutes
CALORIES: 110
NUTRITIONAL VALUES: CARBS: 6 GR; PROTEINS: 9 GR; FATS: 7 GR

INGREDIENTS FOR 4 SERVINGS
1. 800 gr (1,8 lbs) of broccoli flowers
2. 4 tbsp of grated cheddar cheese
3. 1 egg
4. Tomato sauce to taste
5. Olive oil to taste
6. Salt and pepper to taste

DIRECTIONS
1. First, wash and remove the scraps from the broccoli and cut it to obtain only the flowers.
2. Blend the broccoli flowers in a blender until they are almost powdery.
3. Add the egg, grated cheddar cheese, oregano, salt, and pepper.
4. Mix until you get a completely homogeneous mixture.
5. Place parchment paper on a pan suitable for the air fryer.
6. Now, spread the broccoli mixture on the pan, reducing it to a maximum of 2 cm (0.78 inches) thick.
7. Cook the broccoli flan in the air fryer at 200 ° C (392°F) for about 13/15 minutes.
8. Cook until the broccoli base is equipped on both sides.
9. Once it is golden brown, add the tomato.
10. Cook for about 2 more minutes.
11. Once removed from the air fryer for good, let the flan cool slightly.
12. You can cut the flan and serve it directly on a serving dish.

83. Carrots and cheddar potato

PREPARATION TIME: 15 minutes
COOKING TIME: 20 minutes
CALORIES: 380
NUTRITIONAL VALUES: CARBS: 32 GR; PROTEINS:19 GR; FATS: 12 GR

INGREDIENTS FOR 4 SERVINGS
- 4 large, boiled potatoes
- 2 baby carrots
- 30 gr (4 tsp) of margarine
- 60 gr (1/4 cup) of grated cheddar cheese
- Salt and pepper to taste

DIRECTIONS

1. First, wash the carrots and cut them into cubes.
2. Drain the boiled potatoes, pat them dry with a kitchen towel and then peel them while they are still hot.
3. Now, cut the caps of the potatoes lengthwise and set them aside.
4. Scoop the underside of the potato with a spoon, trying to form a cavity large enough to hold an egg.
5. Put 10 grams (1 tsp) of margarine in each potato boat.
6. Dip the carrots into each boat in the same way and season with a pinch of salt and pepper.
7. Sprinkle each boat with 20 grams (1 tbsp) of grated cheddar cheese.
8. Cover the boats with the caps you have set aside.
9. Salt and pepper the caps and brush them with a little melted margarine.
10. Place parchment paper of the same size as the fryer basket in the basket.
11. Cook at 200 °C (392°F) for about 8/10 minutes.
12. If they still don't seem cooked enough, continue cooking for another 2 minutes.
13. Remove from the basket and serve hot.

84. Cottage cheese and tomato broccoli

PREPARATION TIME: 5 minutes
COOKING TIME: 10 minutes
CALORIES: 230
NUTRITIONAL VALUES: CARBS: 18 GR; PROTEIN: 16 GR; FATS: 12 GR

INGREDIENTS FOR 4 SERVINGS
- 1 broccoli already steamed or boiled
- 2 ripe tomatoes
- A pinch of garlic powder
- 50 gr (1.7 oz) of breadcrumbs
- 50 gr (1.7 oz) of grated cottage cheese
- 2 tbsp of olive oil
- Salt and black pepper

DIRECTIONS
1. First, wash the tomatoes and cut them into slices.
2. In the meantime, mash the broccoli directly in a pan suitable for the air fryer; it doesn't have to become a puree, just shrink in volume.
3. Season with grated cottage cheese, tomato slices, pepper, oil and a pinch of garlic powder.
4. Mix the ingredients well and season with salt.
5. Finally, add the breadcrumbs.
6. Stir again and cook at 200 ° C (392°F) until the cheese is completely melted (about 10 minutes).

7. Serve the main vegetable broccoli directly hot.

85. Creamy porcini

PREPARATION TIME: 10 minutes
COOKING TIME: 10 minutes
CALORIES: 160
NUTRITIONAL VALUES: CARBS 8 GR; PROTEIN 11 GR; FATS 9 GR

INGREDIENTS FOR 4 SERVINGS

- 1 kg (2.2. lbs) of porcini mushrooms
- 500 ml (16.9 oz) of half and half
- 2 tbsp of breadcrumbs
- Olive oil to taste
- salt pepper to taste

DIRECTIONS

1. First, clean the porcini mushrooms well with a damp cloth without putting them under water.
2. Remove the earthy part of the stem and discard the unhealthy parts.
3. Then slice them lengthwise.
4. Add a pinch of salt and pepper.
5. Place the mushrooms with the half and half in a pan suitable for the air fryer, and sprinkle them with breadcrumbs and a bit of olive oil.
6. Put everything in the preheated air fryer at 200° C (392°F) for about 10 minutes.
7. Serve the creamy porcini mushrooms while still hot.

86. Leeks and smoked cheesecake

PREPARATION TIME: 10 minutes
COOKING TIME: 20 minutes
CALORIES: 390
NUTRITIONAL VALUES: CARBS: 26 GR; PROTEINS: 13 GR; FATS: 22 GR

INGREDIENTS FOR 4 SERVINGS

1. A roll of puff pastry
2. 400 gr (14 oz about) of leeks
3. 25 gr (2 tbsp) of margarine
4. 2 eggs
5. 3 tbsp of grated smoked cheese
6. 100 ml (1 cup) of cooking cream
7. Salt and pepper to taste

DIRECTIONS

1. Clean the leeks, and remove the green part and the hard outer leaves. Wash the leeks, dry them, and cut them into many washers.
2. Melt the margarine in a pan. When it starts to sizzle, put the leeks, and cook them over low heat so that they wilt without taking color. Season with pepper and salt, and remove from the heat.
3. In a bowl, beat the eggs with the cream and then season with a sprinkling of salt and pepper.
4. Grease a suitable air fryer pan. Roll out the dough and remove the excess side dough. Arrange the leeks inside

and sprinkle everything with cream and eggs.

5. Sprinkle everything with the grated smoked cheese
6. Place the pan directly in the fryer basket.
7. Cook the mold in the air fryer at 200 °F (392°F) for 15 minutes.
8. Check the cooking. If it is not cooked, continue for another 2-3 minutes.
9. Serve your leeks cake lukewarm.

87. <u>Mixed roasted vegetables</u>

PREPARATION TIME: 10 minutes
COOKING TIME: 15 minutes
CALORIES: 70 Calories
NUTRITIONAL VALUES: CARBS: 10 GR; PROTEINS: 2 GR; FATS: 2 GR

INGREDIENTS FOR 4 SERVINGS

1. 200 gr (1 cup) of zucchini
2. 1 yellow pepper
3. 2 ripe tomatoes
4. 1 tbsp of olive oil
5. 1 peeled shallot
6. 2 tsp of mixed aromatic herbs
7. Salt and pepper to taste

DIRECTIONS

1. First, preheat the air fryer to 200 ° C (392°F) for a few minutes.
2. At the same time, wash all the vegetables.

3. Cut the zucchini, ripe tomatoes, pepper, and shallot into small cubes.
4. Mix the vegetables in the pan (suitable for the air fryer) with herbs and 1 tablespoon of olive oil, salt, and pepper.
5. Place the pan in the basket and insert it into the fryer.
6. Cook the vegetable mix for 15 minutes.
7. Stir the vegetables from time to time during cooking.
8. Serve this vegetable mix still hot.

88. <u>Nut and orange sauce asparagus</u>

PREPARATION TIME: 10 minutes
COOKING TIME: 10/12 minutes
CALORIES: 120
NUTRITIONAL VALUES: CARBS: 10 GR; PROTEIN: 7 GR; FATS: 6 GR

INGREDIENTS FOR 4 SERVINGS

- 1 kg (2.2. lbs) of asparagus
- 1 big orange
- 40 gr (3 tbsp) of chopped hazelnuts
- Olive oil to taste
- Salt to taste

DIRECTIONS

1. Clean the asparagus thoroughly by washing them thoroughly.
2. Wash them well, especially in the tips, as there may be sand.

3. Remove the white fibrous part, then put them to cook directly in the basket of the air fryer at 190° C (375°F), leaving them for about 10/12 minutes.
4. Meanwhile, prepare the orange and hazelnut sauce.
5. Peel the orange and extract the juice
6. Peel the hazelnuts and chop finely.
7. Pour abundant oil into a bowl.
8. Add the orange juice and beat vigorously.
9. Add the hazelnuts last.
10. Arrange the asparagus on an oval serving dish with the tips facing inwards, then pour the orange and nuts sauce, and wait for it to be partially absorbed.
11. You can serve the vegetable main.

89. <u>Olive and Swiss cheese tomato</u>

PREPARATION TIME: 20 minutes
COOKING TIME: 30 minutes
CALORIES: 320
NUTRITIONAL VALUES: CARBS: 21 GR; PROTEIN 18 GR; FATS 16 GR

INGREDIENTS FOR 4 SERVINGS
- 4 ripe tomatoes
- 80 grams (1/3 cup) of breadcrumbs
- 30 grams (2 tbsp) of grated Swiss cheese
- 10 chopped green olives
- 1 pinch of onion powder
- 1 tsp of sugar
- The zest of half a lemon
- Oil to taste
- Salt to taste

DIRECTIONS
1. First, wash and cut the tomatoes by removing the top cap.
2. Remove the seeds and put them upside down so that all the sauce comes out, leaving them to drain for about half an hour.
3. Meanwhile, prepare the filling.
4. Pit the green olives and chop them.
5. Now put together a teaspoon of sugar, breadcrumbs, Swiss cheese, chopped olives, salt, a pinch of onion powder and a sprinkling of lemon zest.
6. Fill the tomatoes with this well-blended mixture.
7. Place them in a pan suitable for an air fryer with a few spoonsful olive oil.
8. Place the pan in the preheated air fryer at 200° C (392°F), leaving them for about 25/30 minutes.
9. You can serve the tomatoes both hot and cold.

90. Pumpkin stuffed onion

PREPARATION TIME: 10 minutes
COOKING TIME: 35 minutes
CALORIES: 190
NUTRITIONAL VALUES: CARBS: 15 GR; PROTEINS: 14 GR; FATS: 2GR

INGREDIENTS FOR 4 SERVINGS
- 500 gr (1.1 lbs) of pumpkin pulp
- 4 large, boiled onions
- 50 gr (1.7 oz) of mustard
- 30 ml (2 tbsp) of soy milk
- 100 ml (1/2 cup) of white wine
- 30 gr (2 tbsp) of soy butter
- A pinch of nutmeg
- Salt and pepper to taste

DIRECTIONS
1. First, peel, wash, and cut the pumpkin into slices of 2 cm (0.78 inches).
2. Transfer the pumpkin slices to the basket of the air fryer heated to 200 °C (392°F) for 20/25 minutes.
3. When the pumpkin slices are soft, mash them and mix them with the mustard, the soy milk, a pinch of nutmeg, salt, and pepper.
4. Fill the boiled onions with the mixture.
5. Chop the onion pulp and brown it in a pan with the soy butter and wine.
6. Arrange the onions, and put them in the air fryer, this time at 200 °C (392°F) for 10 minutes.
7. Serve the stuffed onions still hot.

91. Shallot and feta mushroom au gratin

PREPARATION TIME: 15 minutes
COOKING TIME: 10 minutes
CALORIES: 210
NUTRITIONAL VALUES: CARBS: 13 GR; PROTEINS: 10 GR; FATS: 16 GR

INGREDIENTS FOR 4 SERVINGS
- 20 button mushrooms
- 1 slice of bread
- 1 little shallot
- 100 gr (1/2 cup) of crumbled feta
- 1 tbsp of finely chopped parsley
- 1 tsp of sweet paprika
- Salt and black pepper

DIRECTIONS
1. First, preheat the air fryer to 190 ° C (375°F).
2. Peel and mince shallot.
3. Meanwhile, grate the bread into very fine crumbs using the food processor.
4. Also, crumble the feta cheese.
5. Mix the breadcrumbs, the chopped shallot, paprika, parsley and herbs, and add olive oil.

6. Cut the stem of the mushrooms and fill the hat with the bread mixture.
7. Finally, add the crumbled feta cheese.
8. Place the mushrooms directly in the oiled fryer basket.
9. Cook them for about 10 minutes.
10. Cook the mushrooms until they become golden with the feta.
11. Serve piping hot.

92. Sweet and sour raisins peppers

PREPARATION TIME: 15 minutes
COOKING TIME: 20 minutes
CALORIES: 180
NUTRITIONAL VALUES: CARBS: 14 GR; PROTEINS: 6 GR; FATS: 6 GR

INGREDIENTS FOR 4 SERVINGS
- 1 large red pepper with thick pulp
- 1 large yellow pepper with thick pulp
- 100 gr (1/2 cup) of dehydrated raisins
- 100 ml (1/2 cup) of apple cider vinegar
- 4 tbsp of toasted and chopped pine nuts
- 1 pinch of garlic powder
- olive oil to taste
- Salt and pepper to taste

DIRECTIONS
1. First, wash the peppers well.
2. Dry them carefully by dabbing the surface.
3. Place the peppers directly on the air fryer basket.
4. Operate and cook at 200 °C (392°F) for 18/20 minutes, turning them a couple of times.
5. In the meantime, when the cooked peppers cool, leave the raisins to soak in the apple cider vinegar.
6. Once the peppers have been peeled and the seeds removed, cut them into small pieces and place them in a high-sided baking dish.
7. Add salt, pepper, raisins, and pine nuts.
8. Finally, add the oil and a pinch of garlic powder.
9. Cover the dish with cling film and let it rest in the refrigerator, on the least cold shelf, for one night.
10. Remember to serve the peppers at room temperature.

93. Sweet potato omelette

PREPARATION TIME: 10 minutes
COOKING TIME: 35 minutes
CALORIES: 370
NUTRITIONAL VALUES: CARBS: 36 GR PROTEINS: 8 GR FATS: 7 GR

INGREDIENTS FOR 4 SERVINGS

- 4 eggs
- 800 gr (4 cups) of sweet potatoes
- 2 tbsp of extra virgin olive oil
- 2 tbsp of parmesan cheese
- Salt and black pepper to taste

DIRECTIONS

1. First, peel and cut the sweet potatoes into cubes.
2. Season them with salt and oil and mix well.
3. Cook in the air fryer for 30 minutes at 200°C (392°F).
4. Meanwhile, in a bowl, beat the eggs together with the Parmesan, salt, and pepper.
5. Add the cooked potatoes and mix well.
6. Line a suitable air fryer pans with a sheet of parchment paper, pour all the potato and egg mixture, then transfer to the air fryer for 10/15 minutes at 200° C (392°F).
7. Turn the omelette halfway through cooking.
8. The omelette will be cooked when it has a golden color.
9. Transfer it to a serving dish and serve as soon as it is cooked.

94. <u>Zucchini and Swiss cheese omelette</u>

PREPARATION TIME: 10 minutes

COOKING TIME: 16 minutes
CALORIES: 310
NUTRITIONAL VALUES: CARBS: 5 GR PROTEINS: 28 GR FATS: 13 GR

INGREDIENTS FOR 4 SERVINGS

- 1 big size zucchini
- 4 eggs
- 100 gr of Swiss cheese
- 2 tbsp of grated Parmesan cheese
- 1 tbsp of oil
- 4 tbsp of half and half
- Salt and pepper to taste

DIRECTIONS

1. Start by washing and cutting the zucchini into slices.
2. Transfer zucchini slices to the special basket of the fryer and season with oil and a pinch of salt,
3. Once the zucchini slices have been seasoned, mix, and cook for 6 minutes at 200 °C (392°F).
4. In the meantime, in a bowl, mix vigorously with a fork the eggs, the half and half, the chopped Swiss cheese, Parmesan cheese and the pepper.
5. When the zucchini has finished cooking, flow the egg mixture directly into the pan over the vegetables.
6. If necessary, arrange the zucchini slices afterward with a fork.
7. Cook for another 10 minutes at 180 °C (338°F).
8. The omelette must be golden brown.
9. Serve the omelette still hot.

Sides

95. Bay and jalapeno pumpkin

PREPARATION TIME: 10 minutes
COOKING TIME: 10 minutes
CALORIES: 70
NUTRITIONAL VALUES: CARBS: 7 GR; PROTEINS: 2 GR; FATS: 7 GR

INGREDIENTS FOR 4 SERVINGS
- 1 white pumpkin, peeled and cubed
- 1 tbsp of olive oil
- 1 tbsp of chopped bay leaves
- 1 tsp of chopped jalapeno
- Salt to taste

DIRECTIONS
1. First, preheat the air fryer to 180 ° C (338°F) for 2/3 minutes.
2. Cover the pumpkin cubes with olive oil. Then, add bay, jalapeno, and salt.
3. Add the pumpkin to the air fryer.
4. Cook pumpkin cubes for 10 minutes.
5. Be sure to shake the baskets halfway through cooking and check the cooking status.

6. Spray with olive oil when cooked, and serve your jalapeno and bay white pumpkin.

96. __Breaded eggplants__

PREPARATION TIME: 15 minutes
COOKING TIME: 10 minutes
CALORIES: 220
NUTRITIONAL VALUES: CARBS: 19 GR; PROTEINS: 3 GR; FATS: 10 GR

INGREDIENTS FOR 4 SERVINGS

- 2 eggplants
- 2 eggs
- 30 ml (2 tbsp) of half and half
- 120 gr (1 cup) of all-purpose flour
- 1 cup of (200 gr) of breadcrumbs
- A pinch of salt and pepper

DIRECTIONS

1. First, beat the egg and half and half together in a shallow dish.
2. Mix the breadcrumbs, salt, and pepper on a separate plate.
3. Peel, wash, dry and cut the eggplants into thick slices.
4. Cover these slices with all-purpose flour, dip them in the egg and bread them with breadcrumbs (twice).
5. Preheat the air fryer for a few minutes at 200 ° C (392°F).
6. Brush the eggplant slices with olive oil.

7. Put the breaded eggplant in the preheated fryer.
8. Cook the breaded eggplant slices for 10 minutes.
9. Turn the eggplant slices after 5 minutes and when ready, serve hot with a favorite sauce.

97. __Broccoli au gratin__

PREPARATION TIME: 10 minutes
COOKING TIME: 10 minutes
CALORIES: 80
NUTRITIONAL VALUES: CARBS: 12 GR; PROTEINS: 4 GR; FATS: 2 GR

INGREDIENTS FOR 4 SERVINGS

- 1 large broccoli
- 2 tbsp of olive oil
- 1 tsp of mixed spice
- 1 tbsp of chopped garlic
- Salt and black pepper to taste
- Breadcrumbs to taste

DIRECTIONS

1. First, clean the broccoli by removing the outer leaves and picking up the flowers.
2. Wash the flowers under running water and let them dry.
3. Preheat your air fryer to 180° C (338°F).
4. Sprinkle the broccoli flowers with olive oil and mix until a uniform coating is obtained.

5. Mix the broccoli with the salt, pepper, minced garlic and 1 tsp of mixed spice.
6. Finally, add the breadcrumbs and mix well.
7. Place the broccoli flowers in the preheated fryer basket.
8. Let the broccoli cook for about 10 minutes.
9. Serve the broccoli flowers au gratin still hot.

98. Chilli Brussels sprouts

PREPARATION TIME: 10 minutes
COOKING TIME: 10 minutes
CALORIES: 230
NUTRITIONAL VALUES: CARBS: 15 GR; PROTEINS: 7 GR; FATS: 3 GR

INGREDIENTS FOR 4 SERVINGS
- 600 gr (3 cups) of Brussels sprouts
- 2 eggs
- ¼ Cup (60 grams) of all-purpose flour
- 1 tsp of chopped chilli pepper
- Breadcrumbs to taste
- 2 tbsp of extra virgin olive oil

DIRECTIONS
1. First, remove the bottom of the Brussels sprouts and wash them.
2. Flour them well afterward.
3. In a bowl, beat the eggs together with the chili with a fork.
4. Proceed with the breading by dipping the Brussels sprouts in the eggs. Then in the breadcrumbs, again in the eggs and finally in the breadcrumbs.
5. The double breading will make them very crunchy.
6. Roll the sprouts in a saucer with the oil to grease well without excess.
7. Cook at 200°C (392°F) for 8/10 minutes, turning after 5 minutes.
8. Serve this side dish piping hot.

99. Ham and cottage cheese eggplant

PREPARATION TIME: 10 minutes
COOKING TIME: 20 minutes
CALORIES: 340
NUTRITIONAL VALUES: CARBS: 15 GR; PROTEINS: 27 GR; FATS: 16 GR

INGREDIENTS FOR 4 SERVINGS
- 1 big-size eggplant
- 100 gr (3.5 oz) of cooked ham
- 100 gr (3.5 oz) of cottage cheese
- 2 ripe tomatoes
- Olive oil to taste
- Salt to taste
- Oregano to taste

DIRECTIONS

1. Wash the eggplant well, and trim it by removing the stalk.
2. Wash and slice the tomatoes.
3. Cut the eggplant into thin slices as well. Otherwise, the cooking will be too long.
4. Season, between one slice and another, with a pinch of salt, a few sprinkles of olive oil and oregano.
5. Then, stuff the eggplant with a slice of tomato, one of ham and one cottage cheese.
6. Sprinkle the surface again with a little salt and oregano.
7. Place the eggplant on a special pan for the air fryer covered with parchment paper and add a little oil to the surface.
8. Bake 200 °C (392°F) for 15/20 minutes.
9. You can serve when the eggplants are ready and the cottage cheese is stringy.

100. Honey and ginger carrot

PREPARATION TIME: 5 minutes
COOKING TIME: 12/15 minutes
CALORIES: 130
NUTRITIONAL VALUES: CARBS: 14 GR; PROTEINS: 2 GR; FATS: 2 GR

INGREDIENTS FOR 4 SERVINGS
- 800 gr (28.9 oz) of peeled and washed carrots
- 15 ml (1 tbsp) of olive oil
- 1 tsp of fresh minced ginger
- 30 ml (2 tbsp) of honey
- Salt and pepper to taste

DIRECTIONS
1. Beat the washed carrots with a sheet of paper towel.
2. Select the preheat program on the fryer or preheat it by adjusting the temperature to 180°C (338° F).
3. Put the carrots in a bowl. Add olive oil, honey, minced ginger, salt and pepper.
4. Add carrots to the preheated fryer.
5. Enter the vegetable program for 10/12 minutes.
6. Shake the basket after 6 minutes.
7. Serve the honey and ginger carrots hot.

101. Provolone and bacon zucchini

PREPARATION TIME: 10 minutes
COOKING TIME: 12 minutes
CALORIES: 160
NUTRITIONAL VALUES: CARBS: 10 GR; PROTEINS: 15 GR; FATS: 8 GR

INGREDIENTS FOR 4 SERVINGS

- 2 zucchinis
- 60 gr (2 oz) of bacon
- 100 gr (1/2 cup) of provolone cheese
- 1 tbsp of mixed aromatic herbs (rosemary, thyme, oregano)
- Olive oil to taste
- Salt to taste

DIRECTIONS

1. Wash and trim the ends of both zucchinis.
2. Cut them into rounds, trying to make them all the same thickness.
3. Put them in a bowl and flavor them with salt, 1 tbsp of mixed herbs and a drop of olive oil.
4. Stir with your hands to distribute the seasoning evenly.
5. Arrange the vegetables in a special pan for the air fryer.
6. Add a few slices of bacon and provolone cheese between zucchini slices.
7. Season again with a bit of olive oil, salt, and pepper.
8. Bake at 190 ° (375°F) for 10-12 minutes, checking the cooking from time to time.
9. Serve the vegetables hot.

102. <u>Roasted garlic beets</u>

PREPARATION TIME: 5 minutes
COOKING TIME: 10-12 minutes
CALORIES: 80
NUTRITIONAL VALUES: CARBS: 8 GR; PROTEINS: 1 GR; FATS: 2 GR

INGREDIENTS FOR 4 SERVINGS

- 8 Beets
- 2 tsp of garlic powder
- 1 tbsp of olive oil
- Salt up to taste

DIRECTIONS

1. First, peel and thinly slice the beets.
2. Season them with the olive oil and the garlic powder.
3. Place them in the air fryer basket and cook for about 10/12 minutes at a temperature of 200° C (392°F).
4. Check cooking and, if necessary, increase the minutes.
5. Let it cool, and serve your side dish.

103. <u>Rosemary roasted cherry tomatoes</u>

PREPARATION TIME: 10 minutes
COOKING TIME: 15 minutes
CALORIES: 110
NUTRITIONAL VALUES: CARBS: 15 GR; PROTEINS: 1 GR; FATS: 4 GR

INGREDIENTS FOR 4 SERVINGS

- 40 cherry tomatoes
- 2 tbsp of olive oil
- 1 tbsp of chopped rosemary
- 1 gr (1/4 tsp) of onion powder
- 1 tsp of cane sugar
- Salt to taste

DIRECTIONS

1. Wash the cherry tomatoes and halve them.
2. Season with oil, washed and chopped rosemary, onion powder and 1 tsp of cane sugar.
3. Stir well, then place them into the air fryer basket.
4. Cook for about 15 minutes at a temperature of 200º C (392ºF)
5. Serve as a side dish when they have cooled down.

104. Salami and blue cheese potatoes

PREPARATION TIME: 10 minutes
COOKING TIME: 10 minutes
CALORIES: 520
NUTRITIONAL VALUES: CARBS: 35 GR; PROTEINS: 26 GR; FATS: 28 GR

INGREDIENTS FOR 4 SERVINGS

- 4 large potatoes
- 8 salami slices
- 80 gr (1/3 cup) of blue cheese
- 12 almonds
- salt pepper to taste

DIRECTIONS

1. Drain the boiled potatoes and let them cool.
2. Cut them in two lengthwise and gently empty them with a spoon or digger.
3. Put the potatoes in a bowl, and mash them with a fork to reduce them to a puree.
4. Add salt and pepper, salami and softened blue cheese.
5. Add the crumbled almonds and mix to mix all the ingredients well.
6. Fill the potato boats with that filling.
7. Place the potatoes directly on the basket of the air fryer and cook them at 200 ºF (392ºf) for about 10 minutes until they are golden brown.
8. Serve the potatoes still hot.

105. Smoked cheese and pistachio kale

PREPARATION TIME: 10 minutes
COOKING TIME: 10 minutes
CALORIES: 110
NUTRITIONAL VALUES: CARBS: 12 GR; PROTEINS: 7 GR; FATS: 6 GR

INGREDIENTS FOR 4 SERVINGS

- 1 large kale
- 60 gr (2 oz) of grated smoked cheese

- 2 tbsp of olive oil
- 40 gr (4 tbsp) of chopped pistachio
- Salt and black pepper to taste

DIRECTIONS

1. First, clean the kale by removing the outer leaves and picking up only the internal ones.
2. Wash the kale leaves under running water and let them dry.
3. Preheat your air fryer to 190°C (375°F)
4. Sprinkle the kale leaves with olive oil and mix until a uniform coating is obtained.
5. Mix the broccoli with the salt, pepper and grated smoked cheese.
6. Finally, add the chopped pistachios and mix well.
7. Place the kale in the preheated fryer basket.
8. Let the kale cook for about 8-10 minutes (or until they are stringy and soft).
9. Serve the stringy cheesy kale leaves while still hot.

106. Spicy radicchio

PREPARATION TIME: 10 minutes
COOKING TIME: 8/10 minutes
CALORIES: 50
NUTRITIONAL VALUES: CARBS: 6 GR; PROTEINS: 4 GR; FATS: 5 GR

INGREDIENTS FOR 4 SERVINGS

- 500 gr (1.1 lbs) of radicchio leaves
- 1 tsp of Tabasco sauce
- 1 tsp of smoked paprika
- 1 tbsp of olive oil
- Salt and black pepper to taste

DIRECTIONS

1. First, wash the radicchio leaves under running water, then let them dry.
2. Preheat the air fryer to 190 ° F (375°F).
3. Put the radicchio leaves in a bowl, add olive oil, salt, pepper, paprika and Tabasco sauce.
4. Stir to coat the radicchio leaves evenly.
5. Add radicchio to preheated air fryer basket.
6. Cook for about 8/10 minutes, checking the cooking from time to time.
7. Serve your spicy radicchio leaves hot.

107. Tomato and onion eggplant

PREPARATION TIME: 10 minutes
COOKING TIME: 12 minutes
CALORIES: 140
NUTRITIONAL VALUES: CARBS: 12 GR; PROTEINS: 4 GR; FATS: 5 GR

INGREDIENTS FOR 4 SERVINGS

- 2 long eggplants
- 12 cherry tomatoes
- 10 pitted black olives
- 1/2 red onion
- 2 tbsp of shredded cheddar cheese
- breadcrumbs to taste
- 2 basil leaves
- Olive oil to taste
- Salt to taste

DIRECTIONS

1. Wash and slice the red onion as well.
2. Wash and slice the eggplants into cubes.
3. Mix the shredded cheddar cheese and breadcrumbs in a bowl to form the breading.
4. Add the onions and tomatoes to the eggplants.
5. Mix the vegetables in the breadcrumbs to distribute them evenly.
6. Also, add the pitted black olives and mix everything together.
7. Place the eggplants with cherry tomatoes and onions on the basket of the air fryer (without parchment paper), adding the chopped basil and a few drops of oil.
8. Bake at 190 ° C (375°F) for 12 minutes.
9. Shake the basket from time to time and check for cooking.
10. Serve hot.

108. Turmeric black cabbage

PREPARATION TIME: 5 minutes
COOKING TIME: 10 minutes
CALORIES: 60
NUTRITIONAL VALUES: CARBS: 7 GR; PROTEIN: 5 GR; FATS: 4 GR

INGREDIENTS FOR 4 SERVINGS

- 500 gr (1.1. lbs) of black cabbage leaves
- 10 ml (1 tbsp) of olive oil
- 1 tsp of turmeric powder
- 1 tsp of garlic powder
- Salt and black pepper to taste

DIRECTIONS

1. Select the preheat button on the fryer or preheat it at 180 ° C (338°F) for 2/3 minutes.
2. Put the cleaned black cabbage leaves in a bowl and coat them with olive oil.
3. Mix the black cabbage with the seasonings (turmeric and garlic powder).
4. Add the black cabbage to the air fryer.
5. Select the vegetable program and cook them for about 10 minutes.
6. Serve the turmeric black cabbage warm.

109. Walnuts and dried tomatoes stuffed artichoke

PREPARATION TIME: 5 minutes
COOKING TIME: 30/35 minutes
CALORIES: 290
NUTRITIONAL VALUES: CARBS: 14 GR; PROTEINS: 29 GR; FATS: 7 GR

INGREDIENTS FOR 4 SERVINGS

- 4 boiled artichokes
- 6 dried tomatoes
- 30 grams (2 tbsp) of chopped walnuts
- 100 gr (1/2 cup) of cream cheese
- ½ shallot
- 2 sprigs of thyme
- 2 sprigs of rosemary
- A few leaves of mint
- Salt and pepper to taste

DIRECTIONS

1. First, drain and turn the boiled artichoke upside down on a wire rack.
2. Meanwhile, drain the dried tomatoes well and cut them into small pieces.
3. Clean both the thyme and the rosemary.
4. Now pass them to the mixer with the dried tomatoes, walnuts, and cream cheese.
5. Salt, pepper and spread the mixture into the artichokes.
6. Brown the shallot and add it to the artichokes.
7. Grease a pan with a little oil and 100 ml (1/2 cup) of water. Place the artichokes in the preheated air fryer at 180 ºC (338°F) for 20 minutes.
8. Always check the cooking status and, if necessary, continue for another two minutes.
9. Once cooked, sprinkle with a handful of chopped mint and serve.

Dessert

110. <u>Brownies</u>

PREPARATION TIME: 10 minutes
COOKING TIME: 25 minutes
CALORIES: 430
NUTRITIONAL VALUES: CARBS:
47 GR; PROTEINS: 7 GR; FATS: 25 GR

INGREDIENTS FOR 4 SERVINGS
- 50 gr (1.7 oz) of dark chocolate
- 100 gr (3.5 oz) of butter
- 220 gr (7.7 oz) of sugar
- 2 eggs
- 1 tsp of vanilla extract
- 140 gr (4.9 oz) of flour
- 100 gr (3.5 oz) of chopped walnut kernels

DIRECTIONS
1. Put the butter and chocolate in a bowl. Put the bowl in the microwave to melt the chocolate.

2. Pour the sugar into the bowl with the chocolate and stir until well incorporated.
3. Add the eggs, and mix with a mixer.
4. Now add the flour, walnuts and vanilla extract, and mix until you get a homogeneous mixture.
5. Pour the mixture inside a baking pan lined with aluminum.
6. Put the baking pan inside the air fryer and cook at 180 ° C (356 ° F) for 25 minutes.
7. Once cooked, take the brownies from the air fryer, and let them cool.
8. When cool, cut the brownies into cubes and serve.

111. **Chocolate muffins**

PREPARATION TIME: 20 minutes
COOKING TIME: 20 minutes
CALORIES: 389
NUTRITIONAL VALUES: CARBS: 51 GR; PROTEINS: 7 GR; FATS: 17 GR
INGREDIENTS FOR 4 SERVINGS

- 70 gr (2.4 oz) of unsweetened cocoa powder
- 300 gr (10.5 oz) of flour
- 300 gr (10.5 oz) of sugar
- 150 gr (5.2 oz) of softened butter
- 100 gr (3.5 oz) of dark chocolate
- 4 eggs
- 180 ml (0.7 cup) of milk
- 1 tsp of baking powder
- 1 pinch of baking soda

DIRECTIONS
1. Mix butter and sugar in a bowl at low speed until you get a light and fluffy cream
2. Add the eggs, mixing well and incorporating the first egg before adding another.
3. Mix well with the baking powder, flour, cocoa, and baking soda.
4. Pour in the milk and continue stirring.
5. Cut the dark chocolate into small pieces and add them to the mixture. Stir until you get a homogeneous mixture.
6. Put the cups in the muffin molds and pour the mixture inside.
7. Place the molds in the air fryer and cook at 180 ° C (356 ° F) for 20 minutes.
8. Once cooked, remove the muffin molds from the deep fryer and let the muffins cool completely.
9. When the muffins have cooled, remove them from the molds and serve.

112. **Cinnamon cake**

PREPARATION TIME: 20 minutes
COOKING TIME: 25 minutes
CALORIES: 365
NUTRITIONAL VALUES: CARBS: 38 GR; PROTEINS: 12 GR; FATS: 11 GR

INGREDIENTS FOR 4 SERVINGS

- 100 gr (3.5 oz) of flour
- 75 ml (0.31 cups) of milk
- 75 gr of sugar
- 25 gr (0.8 oz) of butter
- 2 eggs
- 1 tsp of baking powder
- 2 tsp of cinnamon powder
- 1 tsp of vanilla essence

DIRECTIONS

1. Break the eggs into a bowl. Add the sugar and whisk until the mixture is light and soft.
2. Now add the flour and baking powder and mix.
3. Pour in the milk and mix until the mixture is homogeneous and free of lumps.
4. Add the melted butter to the mixture.
5. Finally, add the cinnamon and vanilla and mix well.
6. Brush a baking pan with olive oil and pour the mixture inside.
7. Place the baking pan in the air fryer and cook at 180 ° C (356 ° F) for 25 minutes.
8. Once cooked, remove the cake from the air fryer and let it cool.
9. When the cinnamon cake has cooled, cut it into slices on a serving dish and serve.

113. Corn cake

PREPARATION TIME: 15 minutes
COOKING TIME: 25 minutes
CALORIES: 453
NUTRITIONAL VALUES: CARBS: 73 GR; PROTEINS: 7 GR; FATS: 16 GR

INGREDIENTS FOR 4 SERVINGS

- 73 gr (2.5 oz) of melted butter
- 133 gr (4.6 oz) of sugar
- 2 eggs
- 107 gr (3.7 oz) of corn flour
- 140 gr (4.9oz) of white flour
- Chocolate chips to taste
- 1 tsp of baking powder
- 1 tsp of vanilla essence
- A pinch of salt
- Powdered sugar to taste

DIRECTIONS

1. Break the eggs into a bowl. Add the sugar and whisk with a mixer. When you get a light and soft mixture, add the melted butter.
2. Mix the eggs well with the butter and then add the corn flour, baking powder, salt and white flour.
3. Stir with the mixer until you get a homogeneous mixture.
4. Add the chocolate chips and vanilla essence mixed until they are incorporated into the mixture.
5. Brush a baking pan with olive oil and flow the mixture inside.

6. Cook at 180 ° C (356 ° F) for 25 minutes.
7. Once the cake is cooked, remove it from the air fryer and let it cool.
8. Place the cake on a cake plate, sprinkle it with powdered sugar, and cut it into slices.
9. Serve and enjoy!

114. **Muffin with Yogurt**

PREPARATION TIME: 20 minutes
COOKING TIME: 15 minutes
CALORIES: 274
NUTRITIONAL VALUES: CARBS: 34 GR; PROTEINS: 6 GR; FATS: 12 GR

INGREDIENTS FOR 4 SERVINGS
- 300 gr (10.5 oz) of flour
- 220 gr (7.7 oz) of white Greek yogurt
- 4 eggs
- 170 gr (5.9 oz) of sugar
- 130 gr (4.5 oz) of softened butter
- 1 tbsp of baking powder
- The grated rind of one lemon
- 1 pinch of baking soda

DIRECTIONS
1. Put the butter and sugar in a bowl and mix with a mixer until you get a light and fluffy cream.
2. Add the eggs, and wait for the first one to be incorporated before adding another egg.

3. Now add the baking soda and lemon zest and mix well.
4. Pour in the yogurt and mix it well with the other ingredients.
5. Add the flour and baking powder. Mix until the dough is smooth and homogeneous.
6. Put the cups inside the muffin molds and then put the mixture inside the cups.
7. Place the molds in the air fryer and cook at 180 ° C (356 ° F) for 15 minutes.
8. Once cooked, remove the muffin molds from the deep fryer and let the muffins cool completely.
9. When the muffins have cooled, remove them from the molds and serve.

115. **Peach and orange cake**

PREPARATION TIME: 15 minutes
COOKING TIME:25 minutes
CALORIES: 359
NUTRITIONAL VALUES: CARBS: 49 GR; PROTEINS: 7 GR; FATS: 16 GR
INGREDIENTS FOR 4 SERVINGS
- 85 gr (2.9 oz) of butter
- 80 gr (2.8 oz) of sugar
- 1 tbsp of grated orange peel
- 2 medium eggs
- 75 gr (2.6 oz) of flour

- ½ tsp of baking powder
- 35 gr (1.2 oz) of plain yogurt
- 3 small peaches
- Powdered sugar to taste

DIRECTIONS

1. Put the butter and sugar in a bowl and whip with a mixer until you get a smooth mixture. Add the eggs, always continue to whip.
2. Lower the mixer speed and add the flour, a little at a time, and the baking powder.
3. Flow in the yogurt and mix again.
4. Add the orange zest and mix.
5. Peel the peaches, remove the stones, and cut the pulp into slices.
6. Pour the mixture into a baking pan brushed with olive oil and place the peach slices on top.
7. Place the baking pan in the air fryer and cook at 180 ° C (356 ° F) for 25 minutes.
8. After cooking, remove the cake from the air fryer.
9. Let the cake cool, then place it in a serving dish for desserts.
10. Sprinkle the cake with icing sugar, cut it into slices and serve.

116. Vanilla muffins

PREPARATION TIME: 15 minutes
COOKING TIME: 15 minutes
CALORIES: 447
NUTRITIONAL VALUES: CARBS: 55 GR; PROTEINS: 7 GR; FATS: 22 GR

INGREDIENTS FOR 4 SERVINGS

- 200 gr (7 oz) of flour
- 90 gr (3.1) oz of sugar
- 1 egg
- 250 ml (1 cup) of milk
- 1 vanilla bean
- 1 tsp of baking powder
- 4 tbsp of olive oil

DIRECTIONS

1. Put the milk in a saucepan, and add the vanilla seeds.
2. Bring to a boil and then turn off.
3. Put the vanilla milk in a bowl and let it cool.
4. When the milk has cooled, add the oil and the egg, and mix until you get a homogeneous mixture.
5. Mix the flour, sugar, and baking powder in another bowl.
6. Pour the flour mix into the bowl with the milk, stir until the mixture is smooth and without lumps.
7. Put the cups in the muffin molds and pour the mixture inside.
8. Place the molds in the air fryer and cook at 180 ° C (356 ° F) for 15 minutes.

9. Once cooked, remove the muffins from the air fryer and let them cool.
10. When the muffins have cooled, remove them from the molds and serve.

117. **Strawberry Clafoutis**

PREPARATION TIME: 15 minutes
COOKING TIME: 30 minutes
CALORIES: 421
NUTRITIONAL VALUES: CARBS: 62 GR; PROTEINS: 10 GR; FATS: 10 GR

INGREDIENTS FOR 4 SERVINGS

* 3 eggs
* 250 gr (8.8 oz) of strawberries
* 130 gr (4.5 oz) of sugar
* 100 gr (3.5 oz) of flour
* 150 gr (5.2 oz) of whipping cream
* 1 vanilla pod
* 1 tsp of baking powder
* Powdered sugar to taste
* Salt to taste

DIRECTIONS

1. Break the eggs, separate them from the whites, and place them in two different bowls.
2. Beat the egg whites until stiff, then add the sugar.
3. Now add the egg whites to the yolks.
4. Pour in the whipping cream and a pinch of salt, and mix well.
5. Add the flour and baking powder when you have obtained a homogeneous mixture.
6. Mix until the mixture is creamy and without lumps.
7. Wash the strawberries and cut them into slices.
8. Brush a baking pan with olive oil and pour the mixture inside.
9. Put the strawberries on top of the mixture and then put the baking pan in the air fryer.
10. Cook at 180 ° C (356 ° F) for 30 minutes.
11. After cooking, remove the clafoutis from the air fryer and let it cool.
12. When it has cooled down, remove the clafoutis from the baking pan, put it on a cake plate, and sprinkle it with icing sugar.
13. Cut the strawberry clafoutis and serve.

Fruits

118. Apples stuffed with raisins and pine nuts

PREPARATION TIME: 15 minutes
COOKING TIME: 25 minutes
CALORIES: 303
NUTRITIONAL VALUES: CARBS: 33 GR; PROTEINS: 4 GR; FATS: 13 GR

INGREDIENTS FOR 4 SERVINGS
- 2 red apples
- 1 orange
- 3 tbsp of raisins
- 1 tbsp of pine nuts
- Cinnamon powder to taste
- 2 tbsp of sugar

DIRECTIONS
1. Wash the apples and cut them in half. Eliminate the seeds. Scoop out the pulp of the apples leaving only a small amount attached to the peel.

2. Cut the apple pulp into cubes and put it in a bowl. Add the filtered orange juice and mix.
3. Add the cinnamon, raisins, sugar, and pine nuts and mix.
4. Put the apple shells inside the air fryer and add the filling.
5. Close the air fryer and cook at 200 ° C (392 ° F) for 25 minutes.
6. When the apples are ready, take them out of the air fryer, put them on plates, and serve.

119. Caramelized strawberries with basil and vanilla

PREPARATION TIME: 10 minutes
COOKING TIME: 10 minutes
CALORIES: 160
NUTRITIONAL VALUES: CARBS: 36 GR; PROTEINS: 2 GR; FATS: 3 GR

INGREDIENTS FOR 4 SERVINGS
- 400 gr (14 oz) of strawberries
- 120 gr (4.2 oz) of sugar
- 1 tsp of vanilla extract
- 8 basil leaves

DIRECTIONS
1. Wash the strawberries, cut them in half and put them in a baking pan.
2. Wash the basil leaves and then chop them.

3. Sprinkle the strawberries with basil, vanilla and sugar.
4. Place the baking pan in the air fryer and cook at 180 ° C (356 ° F) for 10 minutes, stirring every 3 minutes.
5. Remove the baking pan from the air fryer after 10 minutes.
6. Put the strawberries with vanilla and basil in 4 bowls, sprinkle them with the cooking juices and serve.

120. Figs with rum and rosemary

PREPARATION TIME: 10 minutes
COOKING TIME: 20 minutes
CALORIES: 257
NUTRITIONAL VALUES: CARBS: 58 GR; PROTEINS: 2 GR; FATS: 10 GR

INGREDIENTS FOR 4 SERVINGS
- 6 large black figs
- 4 sprigs of rosemary
- 3 tbsp of rum
- 50 g (1.7 oz) of honey

DIRECTIONS
1. Wash the rosemary sprigs and cut them into smaller sprigs.
2. Wash the figs, dry them, and cut them in half.
3. Put the rosemary on the baking pan, and place the figs on top with the skin side down.

4. Cook in the air fryer at 180 ° C (356 ° F) for 10 minutes.

5. After 10 minutes, sprinkle the figs with rum and honey and continue cooking for another 10 minutes.

6. After cooking, take the figs from the air fryer, place them on plates and serve them accompanied by the cooking juices and a few scoops of vanilla ice cream.

121. <u>Fruit salad in foil</u>

PREPARATION TIME: 15 minutes
COOKING TIME: 5 minutes
CALORIES: 146
NUTRITIONAL VALUES: CARBS: 36 GR; PROTEINS: 2 GR; FATS: 3 GR

INGREDIENTS FOR 4 SERVINGS

- 200 gr (7 oz) of pineapple pulp
- 1 peach
- 1 yellow apple
- 1 pear
- 1 lemon
- 1 orange
- 12 apricots
- 200 gr (7 oz) of sugar

DIRECTIONS

1. Peel the orange and cut the pulp into wedges.
2. Peel the peach and remove the stone.
3. Peel the apple and pear, and remove the seeds

4. Cut peach, apple and pear into cubes.

5. Cut the apricots in half to remove the stone.

6. Take four sheets of aluminum foil and place the fruit in the center (pin

7. eapple, peach, apple, pear and orange).

8. Season the fruit with lemon juice and sprinkle it with sugar.

9. Close the sheets and place them inside the air fryer.

10. Cook at 200 ° C (392 ° F) for 5 minutes.

11. After cooking, remove the fruit salad from the fryer.

12. Carefully open the aluminum foil sheets, pour the fruit salad into 4 cups, and serve.

122. <u>Lemon banana pancakes</u>

PREPARATION TIME: 20 minutes
COOKING TIME: 10 minutes
CALORIES: 212
NUTRITIONAL VALUES: CARBS: 36 GR; PROTEINS: 6 GR; FATS: 6 GR

INGREDIENTS FOR 4 SERVINGS

- 200 gr (7 oz) of flour
- 4 tsp of baking powder
- 300 ml (1.2 cups) of water
- 2 tbsp of seed oil
- The grated zest of half a lemon

- 2 bananas
- Salt to taste

DIRECTIONS

1. Put the flour, baking powder, lemon zest and a pinch of salt in a bowl and mix well.
2. Add seed oil and water, and mix until you get a homogeneous and lump-free mixture.
3. Peel the bananas and cut them into small pieces. In the bowl, mix the bananas with the batter until completely coated.
4. Place the bananas on top of a sheet of parchment paper at the bottom of the air fryer.
5. Sprinkle some olive oil on the surface and cook at 180 ° C (356 ° F) for 10 minutes, turning the bananas after 5 minutes.
6. Once cooked, take the bananas, put them on plates and serve.

123. <u>Pears with cinnamon and anise</u>

PREPARATION TIME: 10 minutes
COOKING TIME: 12 minutes
CALORIES: 204
NUTRITIONAL VALUES: CARBS: 36 GR; PROTEINS: 1 GR; FATS: 1 GR

INGREDIENTS FOR 4 SERVINGS

- 4 Williams pears
- 300 ml (1.2 cups) of red wine
- 200 ml (0.8 cup) of water
- 200 gr (7 oz) of sugar
- 2 cloves
- 1 cinnamon stick

DIRECTIONS

1. Wash the pears and cut them in half. Remove the seeds and the stalk.
2. Put the pears in a baking pan.
3. Mix the wine, water, and sugar in a bowl.
4. Add the cloves and cinnamon and mix again.
5. Pour the emulsion over the pears and put the baking pan in the air fryer.
6. Cook at 180 ° C (356 ° F) for 12 minutes.
7. When cooked, take the pears out of the air fryer, and place them on serving plates.
8. Sprinkle with the cooking juices and serve.

124. <u>Spiced strawberries</u>

PREPARATION TIME: 15 minutes
COOKING TIME: 10 minutes
CALORIES: 150
NUTRITIONAL VALUES: CARBS: 22 GR; PROTEINS: 2 GR; FATS: 5 GR

INGREDIENTS FOR 4 SERVINGS

- 600 gr (21 oz) of strawberries
- 1 tsp of grated fresh ginger
- 1 minced vanilla bean
- 1 lemon
- 1 tbsp of pink peppercorns
- Chopped pistachios to taste

DIRECTIONS

1. Wash the strawberries and cut them in half.
2. Put the strawberries in a baking pan and add the vanilla, ginger and pink pepper.
3. Sprinkle with lemon juice and mix well.
4. Place the baking pan in the air fryer and cook at 180 ° C (356 ° F) for 10 minutes, stirring the strawberries occasionally.
5. After 10 minutes, take the strawberries from the air fryer and place them in 4 bowls.
6. Sprinkle the strawberries with chopped pistachios and serve.

REFERENCES

https://www.greenme.it/casa-e-giardino/trucchi-e-consigli/friggitrice-ad-aria-cibi-da-non-cuocere/
https://www.friggitricimigliori.it/blog/cosa-non-si-deve-cuocere-nella-friggitrice-ad-aria-calda/
https://ricettefriggitricearia.it/cosa-non-cucinare-nella-friggitrice-ad-aria-scopri-i-nostri-trucchi-per-cucinare-qualsiasi-cibo/
https://www.monclick.it/magazine/friggitrice-ad-aria-cose-come-funziona
https://www.agrodolce.it/ricette/
https://www.cucchiaio.it/ricette

Printed in Great Britain
by Amazon